PRAISE FOR

WHEN GOD TURNED OFF THE LIGHTS

Cecil Murphey has been asking me disturbing questions since I first met him as my professor in 1974. Difficult questions can be life changing. The process from question to answer isn't always easy. Yet in this process, Cecil discovers divine strategy at work. He reveals the lessons he learned step by step and, in so doing, offers readers hope and encouragement to get through the times of spiritual void in their life. In an answer-driven world, let Cecil guide you with questions.

Dr. Samuel R. Chand
President Emeritus, Beulah Heights University, Atlanta, Georgia

Darkness. Desolation. Why the delay? What happens when the God-who-is-always-there-for-us seemingly can't be found? If you've ever been in a similar place—or maybe you are there right now—this book is for you.

Dr. Tim Clinton
President, American Association of Christian Counselors

The pages of Cecil Murphey's *When God Turned Off the Lights* read effortlessly. I was both intrigued and comforted to find a Christian companion who could translate the horrid blackness that we all tackle in our lives into meaningful moments for waiting, solitude, patience and, most of all, healing. He beckons us to stop blaming God for His absence and to travel a journey in the pages of this book that offers an easy-to-follow recipe for Christian renewal and personal betterment. This is a powerful self-help book to carry us all through our dark and despairing times.

Rev. Cathy B. Horton, Esq.
Businesswoman and Priest

If you or a loved one feels you're inside a dark deep hole, take a brave step and savor what my friend Cecil writes in these pages of hope. New lights will come on. A new hope will arise. You can be surprised: Joy will emerge. I was renewed and blessed; you will be too.

Gregory L. Jantz, Ph.D.
The Center for Counseling and Health Resources, Inc.

Cecil Murphey guides readers on an amazing journey of faith to a destination that represents God's promise for His expected end.

Casandra Johnson
Minister and Bestselling author

Cecil Murphey has made an exceptional feat with his latest literary project, which provides readers with reassurance of God's presence, purpose and guidance as they journey *through* the valley of darkness and into His marvelous light.

Dr. Benson Karanja
President, Beulah Heights University, Atlanta, Georgia

If you've ever felt the stunning silence of God and truly want to grow spiritually, this book is for you. Cecil Murphey captures the soul of what it means to feel alone and how to redeem that time. With vulnerability and honesty, he will challenge and motivate you to move ahead in your faith—even in the midst of a season of darkness and pain. And you'll discover God there.

Ginger Kolbaba
Editor, *Today's Christian Woman* magazine

When you read the works of Cecil Murphey, one thing becomes perfectly clear: His only agenda is to illuminate the gospel so that others may better understand their walk of faith. *When God Turned Off the Lights* is a candid look into the times when believers feel disconnected from God. Murphey ignores what's taboo and pours out his own personal story of redemption, isolation, revelation and recovery. This book is a gift—the moving true story of growing in faith, even when God is silent.

Bishop Eddie L. Long
Senior Pastor, New Birth Missionary Baptist Church, Lithonia, Georgia

This is a must-read for every pastor, Christian leader and devoted follower of Jesus who is serious about growing closer to God. Cecil Murphey candidly shares the most confusing and bewildering part of his spiritual journey that many are afraid to talk about. He puts into words what many have experienced during their dark night of the soul with wisdom and insight that was gradually revealed by God along the way.

Dr. John W. Smith
National Director, PastorCare

Cecil Murphey has taught us to trust God during the darkest times. Reading this book will help you to grow spiritually and learn to appreciate the blessing of light.

Dr. Salome Thomas-EL
Author and CEO/Principal, Russell Byers Public Charter School, Philadelphia, Pennsylvania

The writer of Psalms asks this question in a time of despair: "Why Lord, do you stand far off? Why do you hide yourself in times of trouble?" (Ps. 10:1). Is it possible that God would use times of tragedy and spiritual loneliness in our life as an answer to our prayer for "something more"? In *When God Turned Off the Lights*, Cecil Murphey reveals the lessons he learned, step by step, in his own times of tragedy and spiritual drought, and in so doing offers the reader hope and encouragement to endure and overcome through the trials of life. This book is a candle to light the way for those traversing through the dark night of the soul, giving hope that there is daylight on the other side of the night.

Craig von Buseck
Director of Ministries, CBN.com

CECIL MURPHEY

WHEN GOD TURNED OFF THE LIGHTS

TRUE STORIES *of Seeking* *God* IN THE DARKNESS

Regal

From Gospel Light
Ventura, California, U.S.A.

Published by Regal
From Gospel Light
Ventura, California, U.S.A.
www.regalbooks.com
Printed in the U.S.A.

This is a revision of Seeking God's Hidden Face, published by InterVarsity Press
(IL: Downers Grove, 2001).

Library of Congress Cataloging-in-Publication Data
Murphey, Cecil B.
When God turned off the lights : true stories of seeking God in the darkness /
Cecil Murphey. — [Rev. ed.].
p. cm.
Rev. ed. of: Seeking God's hidden face. c2001.
ISBN 978-0-8307-5155-6 (trade paper)
1. Christian life. 2. Spiritual life—Christianity. 3. Hidden God. 4. Murphey, Cecil B. I.
Murphey, Cecil B. Seeking God's hidden face. II. Title.
BV4501.3.M87 2009
248.8'6—dc22
2009013214

3 4 5 6 7 8 9 10 11 12 13 14 15 / 15 14 13 12 11 10 09

Rights for publishing this book outside the U.S.A. or in non-English languages are
administered by Gospel Light Worldwide, an international not-for-profit ministry.
For additional information, please visit www.glww.org, email info@glww.org, or write to
Gospel Light Worldwide, 1957 Eastman Avenue, Ventura, CA 93003, U.S.A.

CONTENTS

ACKNOWLEDGMENTS

I'm grateful for the encouragement of my wonderful, longtime agent, Deidre Knight. Thanks to my editor, Steven Lawson, for championing this book. But always, my deepest thanks and appreciation are for Shirley. Always.

FOREWORD

One of the most arresting stories in the Bible is the story of Paul and Silas singing praises at midnight in the stench and stocks of a Philippian prison. Surrounded by hardened criminals and engulfed by pitch-darkness, their chosen response was to sing.

That probably wouldn't be our response. I know it wouldn't be mine! What's your response to a long, dark night when God seems to have turned out the lights on your joy?

In this book, my friend Cec Murphey tackles this question with wit and wisdom. Not only is the subject a challenging one, but it's also a most relevant one. Those of you holding this book will fall into three categories: (1) you don't know the Lord personally, though you may have knowledge about Him; (2) you know Him as Savior and are living triumphantly in the light of His life; or (3) you know Him personally but somehow you have lost that joy of a close walk with the Lord. You seem to live in a valley of despair, or as Cec would put it, "a deep forest, the isolated blackness of night."

Thank God you have picked up this book. *It was written for you.* It will give you hope even when there are no answers. You may ask with the author of Lamentations how you can reconcile your despair and isolation with a belief in a caring God.

God doesn't stop caring. With Cec's unwavering compassion and transparency you'll rediscover that care in this book.

I know something of that darkness. Cec and I wrote an autobiographical account of my auto accident in *90 Minutes in Heaven: A True Story of Death and Life.* In that book, we wrote about my fatal auto crash, my miraculous return from death, 13 months in a hospital bed, 34 major surgeries and years of rehabilitation. Overarching all those elements was the deep darkness of despair, and a seemingly endless night of isolation, hopelessness and depression. Both that book and this one are written for the express purpose of helping all of us return to living in the light of God's glory.

We still prefer the light of God's love to the darkness of God's apparent absence. In *When God Turned Off the Lights,* you'll rejoice in the glory of regaining your intimacy with God. It's not flipping a switch; it's a process. Cec will guide you through *his* journey to a brighter day and help you complete *yours*.

Until we dwell with God in heaven, we'll go into and out of the light of God, just as the clouds cover your yard and the sun returns after the clouds pass. His light chases the shadows away. Until Jesus calls us home, we'll have light and darkness in our lives. Only in heaven is there no darkness, no sun, no moon: God Himself is eternal light, and the Lamb of God is the lamp of heaven. Until that time, we can rest assured that darkness will come, always followed by dawn.

Seasons of darkness remind me of the Arctic Circle. It has been my privilege to be invited to speak several times in Sweden and Norway about *90 Minutes in Heaven.* In those places, at certain times of the year, it never gets dark. Conversely, at other times of the year there is absolutely no daylight. While that may seem bizarre to those of us who live in more temperate climates, the Scandinavians are accustomed to it. And yet, they report that some people become exceedingly depressed during the long darkness. Local suicide rates skyrocket.

Humans, the pinnacle of God's creation, weren't made for darkness. Even so, we must sometimes live there to appreciate the light that follows. Even the most faithful followers of Christ may suffer in deep darkness. From time to time, God can and does turn out the lights. Cec Murphey guides us through the odyssey of light and darkness with compassion, candor and great care, as he always does. This book will encourage your faith.

And we have an excellent biblical model. God the Father turned His head away from His only begotten Son as Jesus hung on the cross. You may well feel at this very moment that God has deflected His gaze from you. He's turned out the light on your life. If that's how you feel, you've come to the right place. *When God Turned Off the Lights* will help you understand that you may have to journey into darkness to find His light.

Jesus is the Light of the World and the Lamp of Heaven. May He shine His light on your pathway. But even if you stumble into darkness, don't despair. Those who have gone before you, like my dear friend Cec Murphey, testify that a brighter day is coming. You can journey out of darkness.

Don Piper
Bestselling Author, Speaker
and Syndicated Columnist

THE LIGHTS GO OUT

The lights went off about 7:30 on the night before Thanksgiving. In retrospect, they had probably been flickering for days, maybe weeks, but I hadn't noticed.

I use the image of lights going off because that's how it felt. I left church after an excellent Bible study. As I drove out of the parking lot, I started to pray. Something didn't feel right. I had no sense of God hearing me.

Of course God heard me, but it was as if I kept sending emails and my server replied, "Error." We lived about a 20-minute drive from church, and all the way home, I tried to connect to God, but I wasn't getting through. I drove through a dark residential section near our subdivision. Lights had gone out for the entire neighborhood. The power company vehicle had arrived and workers tried to repair the damaged lines.

"That's it! That's how I feel. I feel like I'm moving around in the dark." In that community the power line broke. In my case, God simply switched off the lights. I fumbled around in spiritual darkness.

In some ways, that seemed strange. For weeks, starting back as early as late June, I had cried out, "God, give me more. I want more light. I want to grow. I want to feel closer to You." I pleaded in dozens of ways, but nothing seemed to change until the night before Thanksgiving.

God plunged me into a place without light, and I stayed in the moonless night for the next year and a half. I also want to make clear that *God* thrust me into the black pit. Or to use the biblical concept, God hid His face from me.

For months I cried out in confusion. *How can this be?* I pleaded with God for more light; God answered by kicking me into darkness.

When I stumbled into a time of spiritual emptiness, I had no preparation for it and I didn't know whom to ask. At one point, I cried out, "What did I do to deserve this?" Only near the end did God let me figure out part of the answer.

I had been a faithful Christian, and I could list all the things I had done in service to Jesus Christ. But when a man is as miserable as I was, my good deeds and faithful service didn't seem to make any difference.

I felt as if God had left the room, switched off the lights and left me alone. I could find no instructions about how to find the lights or how to turn them on.

Although I didn't know any other believer who lived without light, I read in the Bible about those who felt the same kind of anguish. In fact, that's the one factor that made the 18 months bearable.

I've written this book for those who want to grow spiritually. Although based on my experience, my purpose is to help others when they face the blackness in life—when they want more of God but the lights stay off.

God has many ways to teach us, and one of them is to make us walk down dark corridors, unable to see ahead. We're fearful of falling but we also learn to trust that God is with us even then.

If we want to grow, we will go through periods of darkness, confusion or turmoil. Living a God-pleasing life isn't easy; we're never promised it would be. Yet we seem surprised, shocked or depressed when we encounter such places.

When we can't find the light switch, maybe we need to ask ourselves, *Is this God's way to take me into greater light? Must I first grasp the darkness to appreciate the light?*

—◠—

I pleaded with God for more light;
God answered by kicking me into darkness.

GOD'S HIDDEN FACE

"Seek my face," we read a number of times in the Old Testament. Such statements were God's way to urge the Jews to follow. If they did as commanded, God promised to smile on them. If they disobeyed, God hid His face from them. The Old Testament uses many human terms to explain God. We often call that device anthropomorphism.

When the ancients wanted to speak of divine blessing, they often referred to God's face smiling on them or turned toward them. God's face referred to the presence of God. The oldest biblical benediction recorded comes from Numbers 6:24-26 and makes this clear: "The LORD bless you and keep you; the LORD *make his face shine on you* and be gracious to you; the LORD *turn his face toward you* and give you peace" (emphasis added).

The opposite expression occurs a number of times, mostly in Psalms, where the writers call on God to stop hiding His face. For example, Psalm 13:1 begins, "How long, LORD? Will you forget me forever? How long will you hide your face from me?"

We don't hear much about God not looking at us. We hardly know what to think of God's *hidden* face. "Isn't God always reaching out and making Himself known?" seems like a natural question.

The answer is: not always. Saints in the Old Testament understood. They didn't understand the reason, but they grasped the reality. They often cried out in their pain and confusion for God to look down on them once again.

I understand that experience because I went through a similar period. Maybe you've been there too. Maybe you're there now.

This sounds like a bleak beginning—and it is—but it's also a significant journey we have to take before we truly sense that the importance of God's smile is toward us. If we yearn to grow in faith, encountering the hidden face of God isn't an option; it's a vital phase of the ongoing journey.

Bleak Beginnings

For years my friends used delightful adjectives when telling me about my Christianity, and I loved hearing them. They called me faithful, committed, serious, generous, and devout. They lauded me for my zeal and enthusiasm for God.

But one day, none of those terms fit me; I felt like a spiritual fraud. I kept trudging onward, and at times, I wondered why I bothered. My Christian experience felt as if I were driving on two flat tires.

I knew the right words to talk about God and was good at faking the happy smile, and I doubt that anyone saw much outward difference in me. After all, I'd been a Christian for years, and one of the things we perfect is the holy smile while we repeat the tried-but-trite expressions of praise to God. I continued to teach Sunday school, led retreats and spoke in Christian conferences, but inside I felt dead and empty. I couldn't figure out how to live the joyous, fulfilling life I advocated or read about in the Bible.

I wasn't playing the role of the hypocrite. I *wanted* my life to be vibrant, joyful and committed. I wanted God to smile on me. I cried out constantly for a sense of the divine presence, but it wasn't there for me.

When I closed my eyes, I envisioned God's face turned away from me. I had entered into the emptiest, bleakest period of my life. Intellectually I could explain to myself that it was one of those low points and was part of being a believer in Jesus Christ; emotionally I fluctuated between numbness and confusion.

God had hidden His face from me, and I couldn't understand the reason. I cried out in bewilderment and despair, but no one rolled away the huge boulder that sealed my spiritual tomb.

Maybe I needed spiritual humbling—and I did. God had lessons I could learn only by walking along dark, uncharted paths. The reasons didn't matter then, and I'm not sure they matter much now. I grew in the process. I survived the emptiness, and I'm still following God; so how could I not have grown?

Let's make this clear right now. I don't think of myself as any kind of super Christian or any holy model for others to follow. The best I can say about myself is this: Since I was 22, I've hungered for more of God. And I believe that even the hunger came from God.

For the first 20-plus years of my life I had gone my own way with few thoughts about the important things of life. The details aren't important to relate, but a broken love affair forced me to turn to a source who could heal my pain. That source was the eternal God, and I never felt the "hounds of heaven" pursuing me, as one famous poem puts it. If anything, once my eyes were opened, I raced toward God. I felt like the prodigal son who must have leaped into the father's outstretched arms.

My level of experience has never been fully satisfying—and I don't think it is for any of us who want the most out of our relationship with Jesus Christ. Many times during the years I've cried out for the "something more" that only God can provide, and I didn't even know what something more meant. Then came what I can call the time of God's hidden face—a time of spiritual loneliness and isolation. Only about three-quarters of the way through those dark months did it occur to me that the emptiness might actually be God's answer to my prayers for "something more." Even so, it didn't make that time any less painful.

I want to make it clear that I'm not referring to any great tragedy. I had no life-threatening illness (I never even had so much as a cold during that time); no one close to me died; my financial world didn't collapse; and my wife didn't threaten to divorce me. My life remained outwardly ordinary. The absence of such external pressures or heartaches made my darkness harder to bear because I couldn't find a cause or point a blaming finger at myself.

I'm writing on the other side of that experience. For the past six years, God's smile seems brighter and warmer than ever. This time my external world has changed, but I believe that's as a result of internal events. And I share some of those details in this book.

I decided to write about my months of seeking God's hidden face because I suspect my darkness wasn't that unique. If this happened to me, a rather ordinary believer, surely there are others out there who have wept in the isolated blackness of night and wondered if they would ever see God's smile again. Surely there are others who ask, *What's wrong with me? Why are others living in the sunlight while nothing but dark clouds and darkness envelop me?* This, then, is my journey of seeking God's hidden face.

—◊◊—

The journey begins in darkness;
it ends in light.

WHEN GOD ISN'T THERE

Where are You, God?

What's wrong with me? Have I sinned? Where have I failed?

Even though I knew I wasn't the first person to ask such questions, that didn't make the dilemma any easier. I didn't realize how much the journey into darkness was a significant part of many lives. After I learned to speak with others about my experience, I discovered that a journey into and out of darkness becomes a vital part in the growing process. It's not pleasant, and I hated going through that experience. Worse, it's only in hindsight that we truly value the difficult times we've gone through.

In the midst of our pain and confusion, we can't function with our minds on the eventual outcome. We focus on the present. God doesn't respond to our deepest cries and longings. We wonder how we can keep on when we encounter only silence. It's not that we demand emotional jolts or miraculous answers, but we long for that sense of God's presence with us. *Just a whisper,* I pleaded.

In trying to explain this experience, it reminds me of walking outside on a starless night. We call it "starless" because the most we can see are dark, ugly clouds overhead. Yet we know that beyond the thick murkiness the stars shine as brightly as they do on any other night. Our eyes simply can't penetrate the inky cloud cover. For a time we're forced to live in lunar eclipse, a period of unrelenting gloom. The eclipse goes on so long that it seems like a way of life; it gets tougher and more discouraging to keep on walking through that dark, forlorn night. We know we need to go forward, but we feel as if we've lost our bearings and aren't sure which path leads forward. No matter which way we turn in our search for divine directions, we find only a silent emptiness.

It helped me to think of this from an Old Testament perspective. For those disciples of old, and for me, there's nothing to see because God's face is *deliberately* hidden from us. It may be only a cloud of separation, but it feels like a wall of solid steel that shuts us off.

Even when we sense that it's divine strategy at work, that fact doesn't help much. We still want God's response to our prayers. We don't rely on emotion, but at least once in a while we want to "feel" God's presence or be infused with a sense of certainty that everything's all right in our relationship. Can't we have a tiny nod of assurance that God is orchestrating the night music? Even if God's not taking an active role, can't we get a hint of guidance? A gentle nudge? A whisper? Instead, we encounter only silence, emptiness and more of the lunar eclipse. Beyond the dark clouds, of course, we know God is there. And yet . . .

And yet—that's the problem. God *is there* but not communicating with us. In those times our awareness and emotions don't square with our theological bearings. As far as we're concerned, God isn't there for us, and we can't do anything to change the situation. Despite our agonizing, our groanings and pleadings, God doesn't answer, and we can't force an answer. So for all practical living purposes, God isn't engaged in our life.

Despite all our rational ability and our theological understanding, those dark nights envelop us. We didn't ask for them and certainly don't want them. We feel alienated, and it takes a long time to make sense out of the reality that tiny steps of faith taken in the darkness may be more pleasing to God than skipping ahead on the lighted pathway. No matter how committed we are to God—and maybe the more committed the more powerful the experience—we lose our bearings. It's like being in a state of sensory deprivation. All the outward tools we relied on, such as prayer, Bible reading, Sunday school classes and preaching, seem boring and useless.

I've walked through the dark valley of emptiness three times in my life—and each time it was worse. I'm not talking about doubting the existence of God, and I wasn't questioning my salvation. Spiritual realities had become deeply embedded within me, and I knew, even in the darkest moment, that I was a Christian.

I remember all three times clearly because of the intensity of my sense of isolation from God. I hurt inside, but no one noticed my wounds, or if they did, they had no idea what to do about them. *Why was I the only one who had to go through such turmoil?* I asked the first two times. Or maybe, I wondered the third time, if others were better actors than I was and were able to hide their inner selves so that no one would know—and especially that no one would think of them as unspiritual.

As I look at all three experiences, I can see patterns—which I didn't see during the period of God's hidden face. Even going through the third period of darkness, I made no connection with the previous journeys. Certainly each was more intense than the previous, but I also think that over time we forget the pain and the bad days.

My first experience happened after I had been a Christian less than three years. As an adult convert, I eagerly read countless books on spiritual growth. I felt as if I needed to catch up with the longtime believers around me. A friend named Barry Grahl got me started on the Navigator's Topical Memory System, and within a year I had memorized all the verses. I completed a self-study Bible correspondence course from Moody Bible Institute and read an endless number of books by most of the then-popular spiritual giants. By then I had even read the Bible through three times. I felt spiritually nourished by the Christian community and rejoiced that I had entered the kingdom of God.

Every day during that period I continued to read my Bible and tried to do all the things my spiritual mentors taught me. Despite that, my zeal diminished; I read and prayed less. Instead of going to every Bible study our church offered, I missed a few because they seemed so boring or I felt as if I had heard it too many times before.

What good would it do to keep on praying? I wondered. *Is it worth it?* God wouldn't answer or give me any sign that my prayers had reached heaven. I intensified my efforts and read more and prayed longer. I had to fight the opposition of evil forces, as my spiritual leaders taught me.

"What's going on?" I asked. I couldn't figure it out. I had been living the Christian life and following Jesus Christ. The books in my small library concerned topics such as overcoming evil, growing in faith, persevering in spite of opposition, but none of them told me what to do when God turned off the lights.

Before long I became weary and too discouraged to push myself to follow the spiritual disciplines. At first I marshaled my energy and did them anyway—only to realize that I'd read entire chapters and retained nothing. Some days I said to myself, *I can't read the Bible today.* My prayers dipped to the low point. Everything spiritual demanded too much effort for too little payback. Guilt overwhelmed me and I'd cry, *God, what's wrong with me?*

The first time I experienced God's hidden face, I couldn't talk about my void because I didn't think anyone would understand. So I faked it by continuing to walk through an isolated, empty spiritual world. All the while, God's face was hidden; I had no idea where to search or if God's face would ever shine on me again.

How could I be in a situation like this? I cried. *God, I've been faithful to You, so where are You?*

I ruefully laughed at myself, remembering that only a few weeks before my forced time of gloom I had spoken to a work friend, Jeanette Overton, about my faith in Jesus Christ. She was one of those people who had no interest in God. "I can handle anything that life throws at me," she said.

To Jeanette, I stressed that I served the One who answers our prayers, who guides us and *who's always there in our times of need.* I especially remember stressing the ever-faithful lovingkindness of God.

I'm glad Jeanette didn't come back and taunt me with, "And where is God today?" Actually, for several weeks I avoided talking to her because I was afraid she might do that.

For seven months I felt as if I were in the middle of a deep forest with no light and no discernable path—not even a star in the sky to focus on.

Maybe you've been there. If so, then you've already learned what I had to discover. We search, but we can't find God. We pray, and it's like dialing a telephone that rings endlessly because no one is home. We can tag our situation spiritual depression, the dark night of the soul or any other name we want, but despite our relentless search, God still doesn't appear on the scene.

To find comfort and help, we repeat to ourselves the biblical assurance that Jesus promises to be with us always, even to the end of the world (see Matt. 28:20). Or we turn to the time when the Israelites prepared to move into the Promised Land. Moses assures them, "The LORD himself goes before you and will be with you; he will never leave you nor forsake you" (Deut. 31:8, see also v. 6). In the New Testament we find that same promise quoted in Hebrews 13:5.

Then where is God?

We don't know. We're still walking though a starless night. The silence intensifies everything. Eventually we accept a harsh fact of living the Christian experience: We can quote Scripture at God endlessly, but nothing is going to change as long as God's face remains hidden from us. Until God reappears, desolation intensifies.

So where does that leave us when God isn't around or at least doesn't act on our behalf? We have to do something—at least, my nature is to thrust myself into activity—to get God out of retirement. But what should we do? Nothing works; everything we try seems futile.

While we're going through our private darkness, we're inundated with messages from leading preachers, the gurus of self-help religion and pop psychologists who tell us we can keep getting better, enjoy the fullness of life and rise above our emotions. They insist we can overcome all the limitations in life. "If you can visualize it, you can actualize it," says a friend who's a top motivational speaker.

At the best of times, we find ourselves wanting to agree and to push forward. But what do we do when we can't help ourselves? When we can't find a way out of our dark night? When God isn't on speaking terms with us? That's when those motivational, high-energy messages seem like an opened can of Coke left out over-night—flat and tasteless.

To make it worse, while we're frantically searching for some evidence of God at work in us, friends share examples of victory in their lives. "Let me tell you what God did for me . . ." "I had a won-derful answer to prayer." "I was reading the Bible today and God opened my eyes and gave me a marvelous insight."

Why is God blessing and enriching their lives, and we're com-pelled to keep walking in darkness? Why does God choose to bless them and push us aside?

God's hidden face then becomes one of the hard realities to accept. God hasn't disappeared from the universe—only from our personal world. So it's us—not everyone else—and that makes it even more distressing.

"Where's the God-who-is-always-there-for-us?" we ask but can't answer. If only for an instant, we sense it may be that others are bet-ter Christians than we are, more open to God, more sensitive to the voice of the Spirit, and they're fully committed. Or we try to explain, and the admonitions from our well-intentioned friends sound al-most as if they had stolen the words of Eliphaz and Bildad, who tried to convince Job that he was the cause of his own sad situation.

I thought especially of Job's frustration in trying to explain to the closed-minded Eliphaz, when he cried out about his search for God: "If only I knew where to find him; if only I could go to his dwelling! I would state my case before him" (Job 23:3-4). A few verses later, Job says, "God has made my heart faint. . . . Yet I am not silenced by the darkness, by the thick darkness that covers my face" (vv. 16-17).

Poor Job felt utterly alone and misunderstood. I identified with his dilemma.

In retrospect, I can say that even though we don't know it, when we stumble around in the darkness, we are probably closer to finding God than we ever thought possible. God's absence is felt as a real absence only when we believe in the possibility of divine intervention.

—⁓—

Understanding comes later,
but first comes the long darkness.

4

ON HOLD

Two days after I had installed my new software program for telephone service, I ran into a serious problem. I kept getting an error message and no dial tone. Even by studying the manual I couldn't figure out what to do, so I called the software company on their toll-free number.

An automated voice instructed me to punch a particular number, depending on my problem. I followed the instructions. "Hold, please," came the voice.

I held.

And I held.

After about five minutes, I kept the phone to my ear and started to do other things. As close as I could figure, I waited 83 minutes for a human to answer the phone. When a real person finally said, "This is Yvonne. May I help you?" it took less than 90 seconds for her to give me the answer I needed.

I hate being put on hold. It's worse than a busy signal. When the line is busy, I know I'll eventually get through if I persevere. Or I can call that person later. But being put on hold means I can't move forward in the direction I want to go. I have to place my activities and plans in limbo while I wait for somebody to get around to me.

If you can understand that frustration, maybe you also know what it's like when you talk to God and find yourself waiting . . . and waiting . . . and waiting.

I know the feeling only too well, especially during the periods of spiritual blackout when God doesn't say anything. What else can I do but wait? I can fret, complain or cry out; but no matter what tactics I try, I still have to face one thing: I'm on hold, so I must wait for God to answer my call.

That image became clear to me a few months ago when my friend Mike took me to lunch to talk about the emptiness of his spiritual life. "I've been on hold a lot lately," he said. He spoke of the silence of God—a new experience for him. He had been, in his words, a "half-hearted" Christian for years, but shortly after the birth of his daughter he turned fully to God.

"For the next two years everything seemed wonderful. I'd pray and God would immediately answer. It seemed as if I had a direct line to the throne. I got two promotions at work, and we moved into a new house. Shortly after that, I became the head usher at church, and our congregation elected me a deacon. Three months ago, I took over leadership of the men's group."

He described what happened next. "One day, God didn't answer. Maybe God hadn't been answering for several days. I only know that my life had taken a kind of regular, comfortable routine, which included God. Then the system stopped functioning."

What's wrong? Mike asked. When he encountered silence, he tried even harder and more diligently to get God to come on the line.

Mike faced the same dilemma I had experienced. I had chosen to call it God's hidden face; he called it being put on hold. Regardless, both of us asked the same questions: *What now, God? What do we do? How do we reactivate?*

For several months, Mike went through a difficult time and made a number of changes in his life. "I had to reboot my personal computer," he said with a smile. "The next time I did a dial-up, God answered." He said that being put on hold pushed him to examine his "comfortable routine." For Mike, the emptiness and disruption forced him to examine his life. Most drastic for him, he left a top-paying position to take a pay cut and work for a company where he could do the things he wanted to do with his life.

He said, "I sensed that my spiritual computer had crashed and I had to take drastic action."

Mike and I had spoken a few weeks after I had gone through the third and worst period of God's hidden face. I didn't have enough perspective to be of much help, but I encouraged him to hold on.

After I left Mike, I thought of my own experience that had lasted about a year and a half. Surely this time I could cope with it and find it easier. The most positive thing I had going for me was experience. I'd driven down that dark, lonesome road before and knew that eventually I would come into the light again.

Yet it didn't happen that easily.

Survive the Shadows

Years ago, my friend Joe Meyers went through a difficult time in his life. We met and prayed together. "Look ahead. When you're on the other side of this," I said, "you'll be stronger and more committed to God."

I was in midsentence when our eyes locked. It was only a flicker in his blue eyes, but I saw his disappointment and frustration. In my attempt to make Joe feel better, I had made him feel worse.

"I'm hurting now," he said.

I understood and apologized. Tomorrow, next week or the golden days in the future aren't important when we're in the midst of struggle. Joe, a solid Christian, knew everything I said, but repeating the words didn't help.

Don't we know we'll look back and see the experience differently? But when we're still living in darkness, we don't want to hear—we can't bear to hear—that it's going to be wonderful when the light returns. We don't want something out there in the future: We want something now. If God would say, "I'm with you," or if the Holy Spirit would whisper, "This is the way. Walk forward," we could bear with our spiritual pain.

Once we've passed the big test and gone on to glimpse the daylight again, we grasp astonishing spiritual secrets—and they are secrets—because not everyone will go through the suffering it takes to find God's smiling face again. If we hang on, we eventually come to realize that it's a call to blind trust, and we learn to walk more assuredly by faith.

Gradually, we understand that we'll have days of sunshine, and we'll also experience nights of darkness. We (grudgingly, perhaps) acknowledge that we need them both. Instead of complaining about God's hidden face, we find ourselves rejoicing. At some point—usually long after the ordeal—we look back and say, "Thanks, God, for the emptiness."

Yes, a part of us knows that we will benefit from even the darkest moments. But the feelings of isolation, worthlessness, uselessness, emptiness or failure keep us on hold.

Some people, in an attempt to get us off hold, exhort, "Don't rely on your feelings. Trust Jesus."

Those words sound good—unless you're already walking in darkness. When one person said something similar to me, I replied, "Right now, feelings are all I have to go on. I'm hurt and confused. Don't preach to me about faith. I know God's alive and around—"

"Then trust."

I shook my head. He didn't get it, and I couldn't explain to him. It was precisely because I did trust that I was going through the ordeal. Although certainly not on the same grand scale, I had a sense of what it meant for the Holy Spirit to lead Jesus into the wilderness for 40 days.

Choices

I also knew that even when the darkness engulfs us, we still have choices.

The first and worst decision is to give up. To do so calls Christianity an inoculation that didn't take. "I tried God, and it didn't work." We turn from the faith and go back to the ways we lived before we knew anything about God. I'm writing on the assumption that we have rejected that choice.

The second and most common way is to look inward. "I must have failed," we say immediately. If we've failed, then the obvious next step is to cry out, "Oh, God, where did I sin? How have I failed?"

If we make this choice, we begin to call in the "usual suspects." We each have our list of petty sins and weaknesses, so it's not much of a problem to round them up and force the interrogation. One by one we put the suspects in the lineup. We scrutinize and agonize over familiar territory.

When we concentrate on *our* usual suspects, we constantly call them in, demand confessions and finally give up in despair. Or to put it another way, the more desperate we become, the more intensely we press inward and plead with God to forgive us. As a reminder to God, we may even quote verses such as 1 John 1:9: "If we confess our sins, he is faithful and just and will forgive us our sins and purify us from all unrighteousness."

But what if there is no sin to confess? Or what if we've confessed and re-confessed until there's nothing left that needs cleansing? What if all our frenzied, inner groaning and self-flagellation still ends in silence?

"God, what's wrong?" we moan. "I've confessed every sin I know. I've examined my heart and repented for everything I know or can think about, so why am I still on hold? Why aren't You smiling on me? Why aren't You doing for me what You're doing for all the people around me?"

If we continue to call in our usual suspects and question them, we don't get anywhere. We can't, because we limit our investigation to the known. Such focused attention makes it impossible for us to look at the as-yet-unexamined areas of our life. In fact, we probably don't realize we have such areas in our life.

The third option is to ponder God's hidden face, which doesn't mean that God goes on a trip, resigns or casts us off forever it's only that sometimes God looks away from us. That is, sometimes we may be looking in all the normal places for God, but nothing happens. We can see only the darkness because God's face is *intentionally* hidden from us.

We don't venture into unexplored territory because it's too scary to contemplate, and we don't know anything about what we'll have to face if we do. That unexplored territory is what Carl Jung called our shadow. I prefer to call it our backside. It's a part of ourselves that we can't see. And we can't focus on what we can't see or don't know exists.

The only way we learn about our backside is to hold up a mirror—and, of course, the Bible is compared to a mirror (see Jas. 1:23). We don't hold up that mirror until we know there's something back there to see. And we can't begin to think about the unknown parts of ourselves because we're caught up by a constant re-examination of our known parts.

But it's not all bad.

Such periods can turn out—eventually—to be the most blessed times of our lives. We come out stronger and more committed to God.

—⁂—

Our task is to hang on. We wait until God
takes us off hold and deals directly with us again.

5

WHY, GOD?

One morning, about four months into my walk in darkness, I opened my Bible for the day's reading, and the first verse hit on the *why* question—something all of us ask at some point in our life. It's usually, "Why *me*, God?" or sometimes it's, "Why now?"

"Why have You done this?"

Maybe such questions often get asked because something troubles us deeply, and *why* is the only question with which we seem able to respond. My reading began: "Why LORD, do you stand far off? Why do you hide yourself in times of trouble?" (Ps. 10:1).

I tracked with that despairing writer, and he went right to the core of his concern. He asks why out of bewilderment. It's a way to express confusion, perhaps despair, and most of all, probably discouragement.

Someone told me that the function of the psalms is to touch the nerve of a problem and keep the pain alive. Before I went through my painful, starless night, I wasn't much for reading the psalms. I preferred the historical sections of the Old Testament or stayed largely within the pages of the New. Then my life changed and I cared less about the deeper theological arguments and more about my pain and confusion. I found myself reading the book of Psalms again and again. The writers seemed to hold nothing back in their times of turmoil.

They did something else that I liked. They went right to the heart of the matter. None of this, "God, why did you allow . . . ?"

"Why did you permit . . . ?" They didn't struggle over the old issues of God's permissive or directive will, over whether the devil or evil forces had brought about the problem. They went to God and said clearly, "Okay, God, why did *You* make this happen in my life?"

It sounds audacious—and it is. It's the kind of statement that only those who truly believe in a loving and compassionate God could make. Perhaps that sounds contradictory. I didn't read them as words of anger as much as anguish. I didn't perceive of them as turning against God as much as turning toward God.

Because the writer of the psalm believed in the God whose hand holds the universe and everyone individually, and because he believed that God blessed uprightness and hated wrongness, he could question the divine One.

It's as if he is saying, "Please explain. Why is this happening to me? It doesn't fit with anything I understand about You or Your behavior in the world. How can You stand back and let my enemies and my problems overwhelm me?"

He's not pointing a finger at God so much as trying to make sense of his situation, to find answers when nothing goes the way he expects. Here is a good person—in the true biblical sense—someone who loves God and tries to live faithfully. And what happens? The man's life falls apart. He believes that God blesses the good people and punishes the bad ones, but it's not working out like that. "What is going on?" seems like an appropriate question. "How does this fit with my perception of You?"

To get the power and poignancy of the question, we have to read the entire psalm, as well as examine other portions of the Bible that ask the same question.

Psalm 22:1 begins with the words Jesus quoted on the cross: "My God, my God, why have you abandoned me? Why are you so far when I groan for help?" (*NLT*) The psalm goes on, "Every day I call to you, my God, but you do not answer. Every night you hear my voice, but I have no relief. Yet you are holy" (vv. 2-3, *NLT*). We commonly rush past that psalm because we, as Christians, know it applies to Jesus, and we tend to see it as not having meaning for David in his day, or for us.

Yet Psalm 22 recounts God's deeds of the past among the nation of Israel. "They cried out to you and were saved. They trusted in you and were never disgraced" (v. 5, *NLT*). He looks at himself and calls himself a worm, scorned and despised because of his trust in God (see vv. 6-8). Those are the anguished cries of a person who hurts—and hurts deeply.

Such psalms provided a small amount of comfort to me. I say small because the words reminded me that I wasn't the first to feel as if God's face was hidden or that God stood off to the side while my life went to ruin. They stated the problem; they didn't provide the solution.

In my situation, no one persecuted me. Outwardly my life seemed to go well. But inside I felt frozen and ignored, and my inner pain connected me with the psalm.

The psalms that ask the *why* question eventually move into appreciation and praise of God. They tend to look at God's deeds of the past, turn to the divine promises or focus on God's character. Their poems end on notes of adoration. Yet for several months, I couldn't quite make the transition those writers had made. I asked *why* just about every day. I acknowledged God's past love and believed in God's righteous character, but I couldn't concentrate on those things. I was too busy keeping my head above the spiritual waters that tried to drown me. I felt alone. God's face had turned away from me, and I couldn't understand.

I memorized Psalm 27 and quoted verses 8 and 9 virtually every day: "My heart says of you, 'Seek his face!' Your face, LORD, I will seek. Do not hide your face from me, do not turn your servant away in anger; you have been my helper. Do not reject me or forsake me, God my Savior."

Despite my searching and pleading, God's face stayed turned away from me, and I didn't know what to do. I received no answer when I cried out, "Why, God? Why?" Only silence thundered back at me. God never explained, never gave a reason, never justified anything. I finally had to conclude that I had asked the unanswerable human question.

That's when I decided to move on and leave the why question behind. Two things made the question no longer viable.

Asking the Right Question

First, I asked myself: *What do I mean when I ask why?* When I started to think about the question itself, it struck me that I had asked an *analytical* question when I wanted an *emotional* response. I had probed and begged for an answer to the wrong question.

Suppose God had given me a direct answer to my question. Would it have satisfied me? Probably not. Suppose God communicated to me in some way and said, "All right, my child, here are the five reasons I put you through this." I'm not sure that cold, factual knowledge would have helped.

That's true with all of us. Even if we receive answers to the *why* questions, the facts wouldn't change anything. Suppose we learn why a drunken driver killed our daughter; why a gunman opened fire in a crowded mall; why our company downsized and cut out our job. We might have a little knowledge added to our brain, but it does nothing to relieve the emotional stress.

Second, I formed another question: *What is the* why *question asking?* My wife taught me this one. When we were first married, I frequently asked *why* about her cooking. "Why do you fry eggs that way?" "Why do you put garlic in the salad?"

I wasn't aware of my actions, but Shirley got the message immediately. About the tenth time I asked, she turned off the stove and sat down next to me. "When you ask me why, I feel you're saying I shouldn't do it that way. Is that what you're doing?"

Her words shocked me, and I began the denial routine. Then I stopped. She was right. The only cooking I had known was my mother's, and she did things differently. I hadn't asked Shirley for information; I had criticized her cooking, and it was as if I had said (repeatedly), "You shouldn't do it that way."

As I applied those two understandings to my spiritual situation, I knew I was in trouble. I didn't want information; I wanted relief. I wasn't ready or bold enough to tell God that I knew a better way to do things—although I'd often acted that way. I probably felt that way too. What I wanted from God was comfort. I wanted assurance of God's care. I wanted to feel that God wasn't standing out of bounds, watching me lose the game.

Yet another part of me said, "I have to *ask* the question." For me, it was an attempt to find the road that led out of the wilderness. Previously I had envisioned walking a path that led onward from spiritual victory to spiritual victory. But when I reached the place that nothing made sense, my perceptions became confused.

"What is going on?" I asked. That's the better question.

The old ways no longer seemed to work. When I added the facts together, the previous answers to the problems no longer provided the correct answer. I needed understanding so that I could make something out of the chaos. I had committed my life to

Jesus Christ—many times. As often as I became aware of any failure or holding back, I sincerely tried to get my life back in line.

Nothing happened for a long time.

During those long, seemingly endless nights of darkness, I was
forced to look inward. I had looked to God—and that was absolutely right. But to seek God's face, it also requires an inward look.
We call it self-examination. If we mean serious business with God,
it pushes us to question our motives and ponder what we want.
It's what I call the relentless search. That is, we don't end the pursuit at some high point in our life. It's an ongoing adventure.

God gives us understanding of ourselves gradually—very gradually. To use my earlier image of our looking at our backside, we
can't understand what we can't see. We are only able to hold up
the mirror and slowly see the parts of ourselves that we don't like
to view.

A question came from deep within me: Instead of the mean,
uncaring tone we sometimes charge God with, is it possible that
this time of bleakness might be the most tender method of show-
ing me who I am so that I can become more of who God wants me
to be?

—⁂—

Could it be that moving from *why* to *what* might take us
one more step closer to the light?

6

SOMETHING LOST

Something had gone flat in my Christian progress. My spiritual life had stagnated and taken on a sameness. That's hard to put into words because I didn't get bored with God. I didn't drop out of the church or religious activities, but I had lost the excitement of the Christian faith.

I did the things that any serious, committed Christian would do. Unfortunately for me, those activities had become mechanical. Or some might say it was like following a formality or a daily ritual.

It made me think of the Old Testament Jews. Through Moses, Yahweh (or Jehovah) had given them the laws. The teachers came along and, for hundreds of years, in trying to explain the law they kept adding requirements and restrictions. By the time of Jesus, the leaders had proscribed a solution for virtually any situation they encountered. They had strict dietary laws, knew the types of clothes they could wear, how to plant their crops, even how far they could travel on a Sabbath. The trouble for them was that blindly doing those things seemed all they felt they needed to do.

In some way, my life had taken on that kind of pattern. I followed the rules that I'd heard for most of my Christian experience. Had anyone said so, I would have denied that I operated that way. Only in looking backward could I see how I had become locked into an *attitude* toward God.

One day while reading Psalms, I thought about this verse: "Sacrifice and offering you did not desire—but my ears you have

opened—burnt offerings and sin offerings you did not require"
(Ps. 40:6).

The psalmist wrote those verses during the period the law was
in effect. It surely couldn't mean that God didn't want the chosen
people to offer sacrifices. At Mount Sinai, God had spoken
through Moses and told the people when to make offerings and
what they could give. The wealthier brought a flawless animal,
but the poor could give a bird or flour. Until the destruction of
the Temple in AD 70, the priests oversaw the sacrificial system.

As I read that verse, I grasped the intended meaning. The
people to whom this psalm was addressed went through the religious requirements; they did the right things, without putting
their heart into it. They simply did what they were supposed to
do. But following the rules and living by proscribed methods
wasn't enough. They needed to know that ritualistic obedience
wasn't acceptable.

During my period of darkness I realized how much I had been
going through the rituals. For example, in our church each week,
we pray the Lord's Prayer and recite the Apostles' Creed. One Sunday, we had gotten to the end of the Lord's Prayer when I realized
I hadn't "heard" a word we'd spoken. I had mouthed the words
with the same cadence as everyone else. But for all the understanding I had, I might have skipped that part of worship. That pushed
me to examine others parts of my spiritual life.

Outwardly I conformed, but inwardly I had lost something.
Or the more modern way is to say that I did the rituals *mindlessly.*

In fact, that realization forced me to examine my life and ask
myself, *How many of my activities are done mindlessly?* That is, we do
certain acts and they become mechanical and inconsequential,
and we do them without any conscious thinking. We often focus

on something else and often don't realize whether we've done an action. How often have we checked a lock or made sure we turned off the lights?

In our house, we frequently had to search for the TV remote because I'd turn on the set and mindlessly lay the remote aside. If I wanted to change channels, we had to search for the remote. That is rarely a problem now, because as soon as I lay the remote down, I say to myself, *I have laid it on the arm of the sofa.* Saying that simple statement to myself reminds me where I left it.

Yet, I admitted that so much of my Christianity had been done mindlessly. I thought of the many times I sat in church and stared at the preacher and didn't hear anything—or at least nothing penetrated. I'm glad no one tested me on content afterward.

Several months into my dark night I became aware of my need for mindfulness. As I read again from Psalm 40, I continued to go back to that same verse. Was it God whispering? Probably, but I didn't think of it that way. One thought struck me: *My commitment needs to mean more than fulfilling obligations.*

As I thought about Psalm 40:6, I went back to the statement, "but my ears you have opened." I think the writer could easily mean: "You don't want sacrifices and offerings, and you've enabled me to understand."

Love Slaves

I sensed those words meant something even stronger. A footnote in the *Revised Standard Version* points out that the phrase can also mean "ears thou hast dug for me." The reference is to the "love slave" in the Old Testament. Under the Law of Moses Jews could sell their services to another Jew for up to seven years. At the end of that time they were set free, or they could remain in service out of love for their masters. If that happened, the slave stood up against the doorpost of the family house. With a nail, the master bored a hole through his ear—which is also what the verb can mean. The hole would always remind the slave that he had decided to serve and obey his master (see Exod. 21:5-6; Deut. 15:12-17).

This was where I saw myself before God. I belonged to Him, but I also had choices. One of them was the commitment to be a love slave. I know the analogies don't flow properly, but it struck me that I faced a decision. I was a slave to Jesus Christ and went through the routine of fulfilling my spiritual responsibilities with a kind of mindlessness. I didn't have to behave that way: I could become a mindful servant, aware of my actions, aware of my motivation. I could please God if I frequently checked up on myself to be sure I did it with the right attitude—that I obeyed out of love.

Along with that insight I realized something else: Following Jesus Christ isn't a matter of surrendering so that we can do more for God. It may mean doing less. That was true for me at least. Instead of taking on more projects and duties in the church, I needed to do only what I felt God wanted me to do. One minister, years ago, jokingly said to me, "Cec, you don't have to die on every cross. We don't need more martyrs; and someone has already done the job anyway."

From the context of our talk he meant that I didn't have to try to do everything. Jesus had died on the cross to take away all the burdens, and I didn't have to work like a martyr. Now, years later, I could hear his words to me.

His meaning became clearer as I continued to walk in the darkness. I didn't have to try to do more service. In fact, God was also calling me to enjoy our relationship. Psalm 40:8 says, "I desire to do your will, my God; your law is within my heart."

Then two things became clear to me. First, I wanted to experience a joyful obedience or feel great pleasure in doing God's will. I could do the will of God because it was already in my heart. Or, I think it may mean, if I'm following God, it's instinctual, it's a kind of inner knowing what to do. I don't have to depend on a book of rules or consult with the super spiritual. I can trust God to show me, and then do it.

Second, I realized a sense of having lost something. When I went through the dark period, I couldn't rely any more on the things I had always known. I couldn't pray in the same ways or read the Bible as I had before. I discovered a greater need to be alone and not fear being separated from others.

That felt like loss. Old rules and comfortable habits no longer seemed right for me. I had lost something. *Did it mean I was now ready to find something?*

Grumblings

An abrupt change occurred the week I prepared my Sunday School lesson on the grumblings of the Israelites in the wilderness. They had come out of slavery—centuries of bondage, beatings and deprivation. Now Moses was leading them into a new land. As soon as things became difficult, what did they do? They complained. "Oh, if only we could go back and eat the leeks, garlic and melons of Egypt again."

I hadn't understood that moaning before. Those once-enslaved people were traveling into a new land, but the journey went on endlessly. They had no idea when it would end. People died during the years of their circling around in the wilderness. They were scared.

In their uncertainty and confusion, it was like saying, "We know what it was like in Egypt, and going back to that life would feel a lot better than walking in all this darkness and not knowing if we'll make it."

That's a small part of the way I felt. I hadn't liked living in ritual deadness, but it did have a comforting sameness about it. I didn't like walking in darkness, having no idea where I was going to end up. And, like the Israelites, I was scared of the unknown. Somewhere during those early months, I realized what scared me the most: I was being pushed and forced to spend more time alone—more time with Cec Murphey. The future might be better, but I knew the past. Looking at myself and facing myself meant change, and change carried a sense of losing something.

That frightened me. I don't mean I shuddered; I mean I hesitated and wanted to turn around and go back to the old way. I was scared because I didn't know if I liked myself well enough to spend more time alone. Would I like the new Cec better or would I have lost something comfortable (even if miserable at times)?

I was afraid that I'd expend all my energy trying to get me fixed up and made better, and not like the results. At the same time, had anyone asked, "Do you like yourself? Do you like who you are?" I can think of three responses I might have given.

"Why would you ever ask such a question?"

"Are you getting ready to give me a psychobabble lecture?"

"Of course, I like me. Why wouldn't I?"

The third answer is where I needed to wrestle. In many ways I didn't know who I was, so how could I know if I did like myself? Some of the things I did know about myself, I didn't like. In fact, I found it easier to accept others with their failures and weaknesses than I did the person who lived inside me.

Through the years of my Christian experience, I'd matured somewhat, become a little more self-forgiving and less self-demanding and my attitude toward myself had improved. By the time I began my descent into the dark night, I still wasn't quite able to admit that truth to myself.

I felt like a prisoner locked inside a cell with no light coming in. The walls of silence constricted around me, and the darkness stole my perspective on my surroundings. After several months in that cell I began to look at and confront myself. I finally admitted I wasn't comfortable being alone.

Part of that I could explain. I've taken various forms of the Myers-Briggs Personality Types inventory, and I always score high on extroversion. That means I'm the type who finds stimulus from outside, and, as a rule, extroverts aren't champions of introspection.

While I grumbled inside my sightless cell, I thought, *God has ignored my personality type.* I should have been thrown into a general area with hundreds of people around. I would certainly have been more comfortable that way.

As that thought occurred to me, I actually laughed out loud. That had been my experience. And my past experiences had been inadequate.

Instead of being with others, God pushed and kicked me not only into the dark cell but also into solitary confinement. For a time I ignored looking at me, denied I needed to do anything for or to me. I needed only one thing: I needed God to deliver me.

The longer the confinement continued, the more it forced me to talk to Cec. I looked at him with a new perspective. I thought about him and criticized him, and in the end, I accepted and embraced him.

This isn't one of those things where I can say that I went through five distinct steps, and here's where I emerged into pure sunshine. In this instance, it came about almost without my knowing it was happening.

Acceptance

One day when I prayed, I thought about myself. Days before, someone had suggested to a group of us that we list the things we like about ourselves, the things we dislike, and work on the things we could change and pray for God to help us accept the things we couldn't change.

I didn't write my answers on paper as the person suggested, but I listed them carefully inside my head. My negative list far exceeded my positive, and I knew that wasn't particularly unusual. As I pared my list to a shorter version, there were still things I did not like about myself, and I wasn't sure how much I could change.

"I accept myself as I am," I said several times. Those words shocked me because I don't recall ever having said that before. Most of the time I was too busy trying to mend and fix myself up for God.

I didn't feel like accepting much about myself. When I stared at my defects, I felt ashamed. The more I thought about them, the more I realized that God had always known my defects and failures and accepted me the way I was. But then, God is more loving than I am.

As months slowly crept forward, the force of that statement got through to me. I accepted myself—or at least I moved steadily in that direction. I hadn't lost anything. After all, how important are leeks, onions and garlic anyway?

Instead of losing something, I had discovered a newer understanding of myself. I didn't have to be perfect to like myself. I didn't have to reach a certain standard to be self-acceptable. The matter of accepting myself slowly made me overcome the sense of loss.

Wanting more of God in my life meant not getting more but valuing and appreciating what I already had. I made a promise to myself to get more out of church services. I forced myself to think about the words I sang. I actually listened to the pastoral prayer and punctuated the end of sentences with a silent *Amen*. When we intoned the Apostles' Creed, I read it from the hymnbook and followed the words with my finger so that I could focus on the meaning.

The full transformation didn't happen in a week or a month, and I'm not sure when I stopped feeling loss. I do know that somewhere during that time I became an active part of the worship service. It was no longer a Sunday extravaganza performed for me in the pew, but a participatory experience.

—◊—

I hadn't lost anything, but with my change of attitude—
even while still in darkness—I found a richer life.

7

BITTER OR BETTER?

"Change your attitude," the motivational speaker said, "and you change your life."

That was nothing new to me, or to most people. I've read articles and books and heard countless sermons and motivational speeches that say those same words. However, I didn't subscribe to that theory. Maybe I didn't like it because it sounded like some kind of pseudo-psychology.

Yet the message confronted me frequently. Years ago, I heard a sermon in which the pastor jumped on that theme when he spoke about Old Testament David living in constant jeopardy and being persecuted by King Saul. He said something about David prevailing because he had chosen the right attitude. He applied his message by saying that our attitude is more important than the situations we confront.

I don't remember the pastor's exact words, but this conveys his thoughts: "The remarkable thing is that we have a choice, and it's a choice we make dozens of times every day. We decide how we'll embrace that moment or the whole day. We can't change our past, and we can't control how people respond or behave. The only thing we can change is our attitude." Then he quoted, "But David strengthened himself in the LORD his God" (1 Sam. 30:6, *NKJV*).

The skeptical part of my brain kept saying, *Oh sure, decide that everything is going to be fine, and it will be. Forget the problems and heartaches or difficulties you face.*

Then came my period of darkness. For more than a year I felt as if I were clasping a long rope, being pulled up from the bottom of the pit of darkness. As I neared the top, I could see bright rays of light, and I sensed that God was ready to smile on me.

Before I saw the light, the rope snapped, and I fell. I didn't merely hit bottom; I fell into an even deeper pit than I had experienced before. I lay there stunned, unsure of what to say or do next.

The circumstances that brought this about aren't important except to say that it was a double blow. In both instances, I had prayed a long time and asked for guidance. I was sure I had God's smiling approval. Twice I was knocked down. Either situation would have been enough to throw me, but two of them—one immediately after the other—banished my hope.

What's going on? I asked. *I've already been walking in the darkness for a long time, and it seemed to get better. And now this?*

For maybe an hour one Thursday afternoon, I wallowed in my pain. I didn't want to talk—couldn't talk—and tried to figure out what to do next. My anger focused on God for giving me hope before dashing it. *Why didn't You leave me down there? It's cruel of You to start bringing me out, letting me hope, and then dropping me into the pit again.*

The words tumbled out, yet I found no peace. No solutions. No help.

When I talked to her, my wife wisely said, "I love you, but I don't have an answer for you." When I pushed her for more help, she said, "This is something you have to work out yourself."

I had an important meeting to attend that night. Since I was the president of a writers' organization, I couldn't very well not show up. Somehow I pushed aside my pain and went. I must have hidden it well because no one asked if anything was wrong.

Aside from being the president, I had to attend because Marion Bond West had agreed to speak. Marion is *Guidepost* magazine's most published writer, a friend and someone I had helped in my own early days of learning to write.

Marion spoke, and as I expected, everyone loved her and her message. I listened, but I kept thinking of my own situation every few seconds. On the way home, however, I thought about one story she had shared.

Marion's first husband died from a brain tumor, and she told of her depression and self-pity. While she was still struggling, she sat on the front porch one day and rocked and drank iced tea with an elderly woman she hardly knew. In the conversation, the woman talked about her own bad experiences and said, "Well, you either get better or you get bitter."

Those words had an instant effect on Marion and forced her out of her pain and depression. Years later, I heard the story.

The more I thought about those words "better or bitter," the more I heard them as a choice. Actually I had made a choice before the meeting. I had chosen to be bitter and complain to God about everything going so badly for me.

Now I had choices facing me again, and it became overwhelmingly clear that I could either decide to shrivel up spiritually, feel sorry for myself and focus on all the terrible things that had happened to me, or I could say, "Enough! I'm going to grow from this. I'm alive, and the experience didn't ruin my life. I can make it."

I chose the second option; I would make it.

But more than deciding not to allow those two disappointments to have a negative effect, I wanted it to be a positive experience. I wanted to learn from my experience and be stronger. For several days, I struggled over my dilemma. Life wasn't going well, and I didn't know what to do. I kept waiting for things to get better, but they didn't.

I remembered that sermon of long ago and finally agreed with the preacher's words. I can't choose the situation, but I *can* choose my response to the situation. To admit that fact helped me immensely. That realization forced me to say to myself, *Okay, Cec, if you stay upset over this, then you've chosen that attitude.*

That was painful for me to admit in the case of the way a friend had treated me. He had deceived me and cheated me out of money.

That night when I got home from the meeting, I couldn't sleep. I tried to pray, but that didn't work. I tried to read a novel but couldn't concentrate. Finally, I picked up my Bible and turned to the only part I could feel comfortable reading—the book of Lamentations. *At least,* I thought, *this writer knows what it's like to feel as if I've been thrust into a deep, deep pit.*

Near the end of the second chapter, I found words I could resonate with. The writer complains bitterly about the situation and gripes: "Think about it, LORD! Have you ever been this cruel to anyone before? . . . When you were angry, LORD, you invited my enemies like guests for a party" (Lam. 2:20,22, *CEV*).

Ah! That's how it feels, isn't it? While we're drinking deeply at the well of despair, it does seem as if God hasn't ever treated anyone so badly. Of course, I knew others were worse off, and in fact, I'd been worse at times. But right then I couldn't concentrate on anything except how awful I felt. Sure, it was self-pity taking over, but I luxuriated in it.

Chapter 3 of Lamentations doesn't get any better, because it starts off, "I have suffered much because God was angry. He chased me into a dark place, where no light could enter" (vv. 1-2, *CEV*).

For most of the chapter, the poet's words are bitter, and they ring with indignation against God. As I read them, I thought, *Yes! Here was a man whose relationship with God was so solid that he could actually write and say such things.* "I tell myself, 'I am finished! I can't count on the LORD to do anything for me.' Just thinking of my troubles and my lonely wandering makes me miserable. That's all I ever think about, and I am depressed" (Lam. 3:18-20, *CEV*).

These are the words of a man who was baffled and despondent, and his words reek with bitterness. He says it so well for me. It wasn't a struggle over two serious problems, and I realized that my bitterness wasn't about my outward situation. It was a faith crisis.

As I read the dark passage, I heard myself ask, *God, if You aren't responsible, then who is? And if this is You, how can I square this with belief in a caring God?*

An Attitude Change

The poet must have put his pen down, paused and seriously meditated. When he picks up the pen again, the tone changes. The anger, pain and bitterness have evaporated, and he views life differently. "Then I remember something that fills me with hope. The LORD's kindness never fails" (Lam. 3:21-22, *CEV*).

The poet had changed his attitude. Looking backward at God's guidance and provision enabled him to change the way he understood his present circumstances.

"Well, you either get better or you get bitter." I could hear Marion saying those words. I had to make up my mind what I wanted to do. I couldn't change the person who had betrayed me. I had previously tried to confront him with what he had done, but he kept saying, "I'll pay you. I'll pay you."

I could have nurtured that bitterness. I could have held on to it and reminded myself every day what a terrible thing he had done. He owed me nearly one thousand dollars, which was quite a large amount for me. He had said that he had money owed to him by his previous employer and would repay the money within 10 days. Four months had lapsed, and he had never given me one cent in repayment.

How could I change my attitude the way the lamenter did? How could I say, "Oh, yes, God, because I think of all the good things you've done, I can let this go"?

I went back to read and reread Lamentations. Then I read a verse that shocked me because of the way it was translated: "No one can do anything without the Lord's approval. Good and bad each happen at the command of God Most High" (3:37-38).

Like many places in the Old Testament, the writer reaches right to the heart of the situation. He doesn't speak about what God permits or allows. As far as he is concerned, everything that had happened was by divine direction.

If God sent this deception into my life, I thought, *I'm missing the point. I've become bitter over a man's deception and haven't grasped the message that God wants me to absorb.*

Do I believe that? I asked myself. *Can I accept that God sends everything into my life—even the bad things?* That was a powerful issue for me to cope with.

At first I wanted to wiggle away from such bald statements—and they aren't easy to accept. "God, if you are sovereign, and there is no power greater than Yours," I said aloud, "then nothing happens without Your permission."

No, I wasn't quite there yet. I was still haggling in my mind. Then a small ray of light penetrated my darkened soul. *This is God's doing, and it is the loving act of an all-powerful God who wants me to learn from this.*

I finally asked myself, *Is it possible that God orchestrated all this night music for my benefit?*

For my benefit? That means for my growth. I had to ponder that possibility.

I've condensed this into a few paragraphs, but the struggle went on for two days. Finally I realized I had to change my attitude—and by realizing the need to do so, I had actually changed it.

I was able to say to God, "This doesn't make sense to me, but I am going to learn from this. I forgive the man who did this to me."

That afternoon, I wrote him a letter. In the letter I said that he owed me the money and had promised to repay. I added that it was due to be paid within the next week. I added that the situation had caused a great amount of stress and that every time I thought of him, bitter feelings built up. I didn't want that kind of thing going on inside me.

"If you fail to repay this money within the next seven days," I wrote, "this is to notify you that I will cancel your financial obligation to me. You will never have to pay it, and I will never ask for it again."

He didn't pay the money. I haven't heard from him since. And it doesn't matter. I had changed my attitude; I had gotten better.

Despite that outcome and my change of attitude, I still hated the silence of God. I detested being pushed into situations that made me feel bad, and that triggered all the ugly things I didn't like about myself. I still despised some of the awful things I saw about myself.

And yet, like the lamenter, I could finally cry out, "Then I remember . . . kindness never fails! . . . Deep in my heart, I say, 'The

LORD is all I need; I can depend on him!' " (Lam. 3:21-22,24, *CEV*).

I was beginning to understand and to get better.

How Long?

If the spiritual silence continues long enough, eventually we cry out, "How long, O Lord? How long do I have to keep pleading and You don't respond?"

After weeks of walking in a starless night, I prayed, *How long is the darkness going to keep on? How long do I have to stumble in darkness and pain? How long will You hide Your face from me?*

Those questions took me beyond the *why* question. By then I had accepted that I didn't need reasons (and God probably wasn't going to explain anyway).

"That's the way it is," I said, and I tried to console myself by thinking of spiritual growth, maturing in my relationship with God and persevering in the good fight of faith. As the ordeal continued, a spiritual weariness descended over me. I grew tired of waiting and felt worn out from living with no sense of divine guidance.

Although I didn't recognize it, the asking of *how long* took me forward in my seeking God's hidden face in my journey out of darkness.

How long will this go on? That wasn't a question arising merely from curiosity but from something that emerged from the depth of my soul. "Is it going to last the rest of my life?" Even as I said those words, I knew it wouldn't.

And yet, one morning, I reached the place where it seemed as if the darkness would pursue me to the grave. No matter how much I went through the usual methods of prayer or how fervently I looked inwardly, nothing changed.

That particular morning I began with Psalm 1, which is short, and then I started Psalm 2, and I had to force myself to get past the fourth verse. I kept on. Most of the time I read words that held no meaning for me. I might as well have been reading in Urdu. But when I reached Psalm 13, I felt as if my eyes had suddenly opened. Here was a man asking the same questions. Strange, but all the times I'd read Psalm 13 before, I had scarcely paid any attention to the deep-seated pain of the writer.

I suppose I thought of someone praying and saying, "Lord, I'm waiting for you to answer prayer." I envisioned someone writing in the midst of battle, with enemies all around, and waiting for deliverance from God.

This time the words sounded as if they were *my* words—and they welled up from a deep, despairing pit. My life wasn't in danger, and nothing terrible confronted me—at least outwardly. Yet as I read those first two verses, they hit me.

"How long, LORD? Will you forget me forever? How long will you hide your face from me? How long must I wrestle with my thoughts and day after day have sorrow in my heart? How long will my enemy triumph over me?" (Ps. 13:1-2).

Another version brought it even closer to me: "How much longer, LORD, will you forget about me? Will it be forever? How long will you hide?" (Ps. 13:1-2, *CEV*).

The psalm writer's circumstances differed from mine, but we both cried from the same kind of pain. The poet understood his condition, and as I read those words, I felt his timeless words spoke as if they were mine. I no longer felt like an alien on planet earth. Someone else had lived with the same inner turmoil.

I have no idea how many times over the next month I turned to and read those two verses—it must have been at least five times each day and in several translations. The repetition of the verses didn't give me answers, and I didn't see any light along the path but through the words on the page. I had met a kindred soul. *He has been there. He knows what it's like to walk alone in a strange kind of unending darkness.*

I continued to ponder those two verses. Four times, David (or whoever wrote the psalm) penned the same plaintive wail that echoed from my heart: "How long? How long?"

Perhaps it's an eternal human cry, one that all sincere believers have to ask at some phase in their life. It's a cry that comes from the brink of despair and says, "I'm weak and helpless. How long do I have to keep hanging on before You deliver me?"

When the psalmist asks, "Will you forget me forever? How long will you hide your face from me?" he writes out of his emotional reaction, but I'm convinced he didn't believe that God had abandoned him or forgotten him in his troubles. He didn't mean that God no longer remembered, didn't know or care about, his circumstances. On the contrary, I think the poet made it clear that he believed God had put him where he was. And yet now he cried out as if God had forgotten.

God Remembers

Someone once told me that when we read the words "forgetting," "remembering," and "seeing" applied to God, they're not statements or complaints about the lack of divine consciousness; they are pleas for divine action. It's a way of saying, "Lord, haven't I suffered enough? Isn't it time for you to come to my rescue?"

A good example of the matter of God remembering appears in Exodus concerning the ordeal of the Jews in Egypt. Long after the death of Joseph, the people became slaves, and their situation grew more and more intolerable. "God heard their groaning and he remembered his covenant with Abraham, with Isaac and with Jacob. So God looked on the Israelites and was concerned about them" (Exod. 2:24-25).

Because they had lived in slavery and with such desperate needs for so long, it was as if God had forgotten. For the writer to say, "God remembered his covenant" is a word to encourage the people more than it is to speak about God. They perceived the lack of divine action as if God had forgotten them.

Something else—and it may seem obvious—is that whenever we read the biblical statement, "God remembered," and we continue reading, we grasp that those two words are a prelude for divine intervention.

In Psalm 13, David didn't think God had lost track of him. If that's true, what did he mean? Why would he bother to cry out? As I continued to read the psalm, I received comfort in knowing that someone else had lived in darkness for a long time. Someone else had cried out with a voice of weariness.

Maybe a better way to think of David's questions is to say that "How long, O God?" isn't the real question. In his difficulties, the man is saying, "God, I'm alone. No one is here to help me, and You're the only one to whom I can turn. Please help me and take me out of this. If You don't come to my aid—and come soon—I'm finished. I can't hold out much longer."

Psalm 13 is one of several instances where the psalmist yearns to see God's face, but he means more than being in God's presence. He wants help. Encouragement. Comfort.

In Psalm 13:2, he cries out, "Day after day [I] have sorrow in my heart" or, as another version translates it, "pain in my soul." He isn't asking God to tell him, "One more week and then I'll stop."

The question carries more the idea of "How much more of this must I endure? What has to happen before You deliver me?"

Only those who have felt the black emptiness that goes on and on grasp the anguish of this cry: "There must be an end, and I know it will happen; but please, please bring it about soon."

Another thing that reading Psalm 13 did for me was to help me realize I was in good spiritual company. If the great believer and spiritual champion, David, cried out in such despair, maybe I was on the right track after all.

And like other psalms that cry out to see the face of God, Psalm 13 also ends on a note of hope: "I will sing to the LORD, because he has dealt bountifully with me" (v. 6, *RSV*).

David found hope by looking backward at the divine blessings and faithfulness. God hadn't failed him in the past, and that gave him confidence to believe in the same unfailing guidance for the days ahead. That's the real song of praise that ends this psalm, as if to say, "Things are terrible, but I know from past experiences this isn't the end. You are going to deliver me because that's what You've always done."

Thousands of years after the origin of the verses, I had the same sense of knowing it as well.

—◈—

One day God would make my eyes sparkle again,
but I had no idea when.

8

BEWILDERED BY THE DARKNESS

How do you run away when there's no place to go? How do you escape the darkness when no light shines enough to show you which path to take?

Too often we think that if we could escape the immediate situation, life would be smooth and uneventful. It wouldn't be—we'd soon be involved in another crisis. Or we think, "If only my circumstances could be different." Even at my lowest moments I realized that doing things such as finding new friends or joining a different church would solve nothing.

It took me a long time to realize that it isn't the *outward* circumstances that give us the trouble anyway. Our problems arise out of who we are. The same problems will find us no matter where we run, although they come in different forms.

Running is the easy way. Sometimes we wish we could go back to an earlier time in our life when everything seemed simple and problem free. (It probably never was, we only remember it that way.) We change jobs, join another church, move out of our neighborhood, resign from organizations, but the problems—often the same problems—follow us. We can't outrun ourselves.

During my dark period and my reading of Psalms, I found some help from Psalm 11. I identified with the poet's emotions, even though I didn't understand his actual circumstances. "In the

LORD I put my trust: How can you say to my soul, 'Flee as a bird to your mountain'? For look! The wicked bend their bow, they make ready their arrow on the strong, that they may shoot secretly at the upright in heart" (vv. 1-2, *NKJV*).

The first word in Hebrew is "LORD" (Yahweh or Jehovah) because it emphasizes where the poet seeks refuge. This makes it clear from the first word that the writer seeks Yahweh and not another god or human source. Obvious? Maybe, but in my state of mind, I needed to keep pulling myself back to the basics—utter reliance on God.

As I read the psalm through several times, I kept pausing over the word "flee." At the moment, to run away sounded appealing. While I continued to walk in darkness, I wanted to escape from my circumstances.

The writer also says that the unrighteous "have fitted their arrow . . . to shoot in the dark at the upright in heart" (v. 2, *RSV*). Scholars have trouble translating verse 2. The Hebrew has a number of words for "darkness." This particular one doesn't speak of night or a dark night. It carries a more symbolic meaning. When I discussed this psalm with a scholarly friend, he said, "It's the darkness of the soul's despair; it's the gloom of Sheol [place of the dead], and it often leads to depression."

Don't Run Away

I understood the emotions that writer wanted to convey. He's urging us not to flee from the place or try to avoid the experience in which God has placed us. It's exactly there—right in the midst of that terrible chaos or pain—where God intends us to be. It is there that our commitment (or lack of it) shows.

The writer goes on to make it clear that God works from "his holy temple, the LORD's throne is in heaven" (11:4, *RSV*). That's where we need to flee—into God's presence.

I read the psalm carefully, I accepted and believed it. "Tell me how," I pleaded. "How do I turn to God's holy temple when I can't see anything but an overwhelming darkness? Where are You? Where is Your temple?"

The silent darkness continued to engulf me. No matter what I read, I was seeking a way to run away from the darkness. Even though I realized the importance of the enforced silence, the absence of light, I still didn't like it.

As I got to the end of the psalm, I actually felt greater frustration. The writer ends with these words: "For the LORD is righteous, he loves righteous deeds; the upright shall behold his face" (11:7, *RSV*). Apparently, he has resolved his problem. He cried out, God answered and he could speak of beholding God's face.

No bells rang and no bright insight penetrated my thinking. In the first verses, I had resonated with the writer's emotions and felt a yearning for the same answers he sought. He had put into words exactly what I wanted—to behold God's face once again.

But how, God? I prayed. I couldn't put on a fake grin and move forward, because I still had no answers. "How do I find Your face that's hidden from me by darkness?"

The Lingering Darkness

Despite my persistent asking, the darkness lingered. I had no signs that the situation would improve, but I did have a promise from God, and I tried to fasten on to that. The words of Psalm 11 encouraged me that if I lived a life of doing "righteous deeds," the day would come when I wouldn't have to struggle to see what had been God's hidden face. I'd be able to experience the smile from heaven on me.

Somewhere in my darkness I thought of others who prayed difficult prayers from earnest hearts. They were in dark places, and they came through them. For example, I focused on the story of Elijah praying for rain. It hadn't rained in Israel for three and a half years because the prophet himself had prayed and asked God to hold the rain back. Now he asks God to send the rain once again. He prays and nothing happens. Elijah sends his servant out to look at the clouds (see 1 Kings 18:44). The man comes back and says the skies are cloudless.

Does Elijah stop praying? Of course not. He prays again and then says, "Go back and look at the face of heaven" (my paraphrase). He looks and sees nothing. "Go back again." The seventh time, the man returns to Elijah and says, "I saw a cloud, a tiny cloud. Why, it's so small that it's only about the size of a man's hand."

"That's it!" For Elijah that tiny cloud on the edge of the horizon is enough. He starts racing down the mountain, and the deluge hits before he reaches the bottom.

It's a wonderful story. The comfort I found from reading it again was that Elijah went into action when he had only the tiniest fragment of evidence.

I knew then what I had to do: wait and pray. It might take 7 times or 70, but I had committed myself. I would wait. I had no choice, of course, but reading those verses from the psalm strengthened me to say, "I'll wait. It will happen."

It happened, but not for a long, long time. As I persisted in praying for light to burst through, sometimes I felt like Elijah's servant rushing out to gaze at the cloudless sky. "Nothing yet," I'd have to say.

The waiting, the looking, the praying—those were the things I could understand.

During that phase of the dark night without seeing God's face, my usual Bible reading, along with the book of Psalms, was the small book of Lamentations, most often in a modern translation. The pathos of the writer's words and situation gripped me. I felt as if I sat next to him as he poured out his words.

Of course our situations differed greatly. This is a book of sorrows or laments about the destruction of Jerusalem. He writes about people who had sinned and repeatedly turned their backs on God. Despite warnings and the prophet's predictions of defeat and persecution, the people had continued on their downward path. As sad as their situation was—and some of the details are heart wrenching—they deserved what they got.

As he writes, it's a terrible time of darkness for them. But there is the first hint of understanding their dilemma. "The LORD has punished Jerusalem because of her awful sins; he has let her people be dragged away" (Lam. 1:5, CEV).

As I thought about the first lament, I sensed their confusion. Most of the verses in chapter 1 describe the situation and plead for God's grace, but there's little of the anger or punishment of God involved.

Then I read, "The LORD was right, but I refused to obey him" (Lam. 1:18, CEV).

Confused

Before I got to the point of their sinfulness, I stayed in the mood of confusion. I felt like a dazed man who walks down the street shaking his head, trying to bring sense into what's going on in his world. It was as if the writer is saying, "I'm here, and everything is wrong, and I can't figure out how it happened."

I paused then and remembered an accident in which I was involved. I was teaching at a writers' conference in Orlando, Florida.

A few minutes before 5:00 in the morning I went for my morning run. I recall looking at my watch at 5:05 before I started to cross a wide intersection. A car approached from the right, and he had a red light. He didn't stop. Instead he made a U-turn right in front of me. When I looked up, the car was only feet away. The metal struck my outstretched hands.

At 5:35, someone let me out of a car in front of the Holiday Inn and asked, "Are you sure you're all right?"

I said I was. I walked inside, found the men's room and vomited. Blood streaked down the back of my head. (Fortunately I had no serious effects from the accident, and eventually I did see a doctor.) I couldn't remember anything that happened from the moment of impact until I got out of the car in the parking lot.

The point of my story is that I had lost half an hour of my life. I walked to my room and lay down. At the time I felt no pain but only a terrible confusion. What had happened? Thirty minutes of my life had flown away, and I couldn't remember or explain them. Someone must have picked me up and helped me into the car. Was it the driver of the car that hit me? Did someone else see me lying on the street and pick me up?

One minute I had been running; the next conscious moment, half an hour had lapsed. I'll never know the answer to what happened. I had to accept the dazed confusion and go on with my life.

As I read the first chapter of Lamentations again and again, I had the sense that bewilderment was still another step beyond asking, "Why, God? Why me?" For me, it meant I had to accept the reality of my situation; I simply didn't understand it, but that didn't mean I couldn't acknowledge that it had happened to me.

In the first days after God sent the darkness into my life, I had been convinced that I had done some awful sin, otherwise why would God have turned off the lights? I felt worthless and unworthy, constantly questioning my motives and thoughts. I progressed to the place where I finally believed that whatever was going on—whatever was separating me from God's presence—wasn't caused by my wrongdoing or sinfulness.

Bewildered

I had reached the stage of bewilderment. It's not a time of answers, but it is one step toward coming out of the darkness, even though I didn't realize it.

I'm not sure I can put into words what went on inside me. If I could have found a deep-seated sin, I could have said, "Yes, God, this is exactly what I deserve. In fact, I probably deserve more." The darkness would have made sense. I discerned no serious sin and certainly had no awareness of any deliberate disobedience. Or if I could have found evil motives even when I did good things, I could have found some comfort. *Oh yes, God, You've forced me to look inward and see that my intentions have been selfish. I've cloaked them with the garb of goodness, and others didn't see. But You did.*

Yet no amount of self-examination, prayer or reading the Bible brought any such conclusion.

Yes, I struggled, and at one point I even accused myself of self-delusion. Was I blinded by my own sinfulness? Did I refuse to see what I didn't want to see? Had I justified myself so that I didn't have to face my wrongdoing? Again nothing came from that rigorous self-examination.

That brought me back to bewilderment.

If it's not sin, impure motives or self-deception, then what is it? I felt as if I had walked into a theater in the middle of act two and had no idea what had gone on before or what would take place in act three. Nothing made much sense. In desperation, I turned to Psalm 139 and read: "Look deep into my heart, God, and find out everything I am thinking. Don't let me follow evil ways, but lead me in the way that time has proven true" (vv. 23-24, *CEV*).

My confusion didn't go away. Nothing made sense yet. However, I did resolve that I would accept the parts of my life, like the missing 30 minutes, that didn't make sense.

In the midst of my confusion I didn't know what to do. I repeated those two verses from Psalm 139 and read them from several translations. "God, this is my prayer. It's as honest and as sincere as I know how to be."

The old voice within me that often whispered condemnation went silent. The inner critic who laughed when I talked about sincerity turned mute. No fingers of guilt grabbed me by the throat—only bewilderment and darkness.

What's going on? What am I doing in a place like this?

In the middle of all that confusion I sensed that I had moved forward, even though I couldn't explain to myself what forward meant or how I knew.

The bewilderment gave way—gradually—to acceptance. Probably for the first time I admitted I couldn't do anything to change the situation. Darkness was still everywhere, and it was going to stay until God's appointed moment for the sunshine to burst forth.

—◊◊◊—

I had begun to develop the ability
to see the right direction to go.

9

COMPLACENCY

If anyone had ever charged me with becoming complacent in my Christian experience, I would have scoffed or laughed. "Life has too many ups and downs for complacency to set in," I would have said. "Too many times I have to cry out for guidance or try to figure out what to do."

And yet I've come to believe—because of personal experience—that complacency can set in. No, I'll say it more strongly. I have experienced complacency, and I know that a sense of self-satisfaction can happen to any of us who try to live a faithful and committed life. We become involved in many activities: prayer, reading our Bibles and other books, involving ourselves in our church and in serving others. Yet even that lifestyle can make us feel self-satisfied, maybe even smug. It's subtle, but that doesn't make it less real.

Frankly, because I hadn't ever thought complacency would describe me, I didn't consider it until two things happened. First was the silence of God. Second, someone sent me a quotation by email without attributing the source: "Easy circumstances and a careless outlook are seldom far apart."

When I first read the clever saying, I nodded and agreed, and realized it didn't apply to me, although I kept the quotation on my hard drive. Yet in the midst of my silence, I began to examine the possibility. I went back and read the words aloud several times. I had begun to see many things differently in my life and I didn't want to ignore any possibility.

My lifestyle had often been filled with the voice of Nathan, the prophet of old, echoing through the centuries. He had denounced David for his sin with Bathsheba and cried out, "You are the man!" (2 Sam. 12:7).

I understood the shame and the terrible embarrassment of being found out. But what should I do when I couldn't conjure up failings, sins or impure motives?

Or was that message something I needed to absorb? Had I grown smug? Fallen into a routine? Allowed my zeal to diminish? As difficult as it was for me, I finally had to admit, "Yes, that describes me." But almost immediately I defended myself by saying, "I didn't mean for it to happen."

During that period, I reflected on something our pastor of many years ago, Brother Broker, had warned about. When things are going too well, we face greater spiritual danger than when our lives seem upset and torn apart. I listened to his exhortation and assented but didn't think much about it. I'm not sure why those words remained in my memory all through the years. At the time, *he* was in turmoil and resigned only a few months later. It was one of those instances when I believed he preached more to himself than to us. Consequently I easily pushed its relevance aside.

So why did those words stay with me? Could it be that it was a message I needed to hear, but I wasn't ready? For nearly 30 years those words remained in a corner of my brain, waiting for me to recall them.

Through the years, between the pastor's message and that email, I've heard that kind of talk dozens of times. I didn't like hearing such messages. Furthermore, I disagreed with them. Self-satisfaction could happen to anyone but not to those who were faithful. I rejected such a possibility for me because of my commitment to an idea expressed in six words: obedience brings blessings; disobedience brings troubles. And if I obey God each day, what else is there?

Certainly I was in good company with the general thinking that I read in the Old Testament. The promise was there of long life, many children and prosperity if the people followed God. Their disobedience hurled divine curses on their heads.

It didn't always work that way. The most obvious case is poor Job. He was a righteous man, and everything went wrong in his life. His "comforting" friends admitted they couldn't discern any outward sin in his life, so his disobedience must have been inward, and if he would confess, God would forgive him.

Almost everyone knows that Job is the exception, and anyway, all the troubles and trials came about because of the devil's demands.

In some ways, we still live by the limited Old Testament concept. If good things happen, we're living right. If things go bad, sour or tragic, God is punishing us for our failures. As soon as life takes a bad turn, the first question some of our friends push us to ask ourselves is, "What did I do wrong?"

There must be a reason, and I'm the obvious reason. I think that is a good place to start. It doesn't mean self-flagellating with cords of shame or guilt. We start there, and then we move on. It's like the time the doctor sent my wife for an MRI to rule out a brain tumor when she suffered from severe headaches. Sometimes we have to figure out what *isn't* wrong before we can work on what *is*.

Suppose we search our heart, and we sincerely have no sense of failure or disobedience. Then what do we do?

Or coming at it from another perspective, what happens when everything goes smoothly? What does it mean when we're financially prosperous, have a stable family, a circle of happy relationships and feel respected by our community?

Even though I hate to admit it, I think Brother Broker had it right. When life goes smoothly, we tend to get careless. We take things for granted. "This is the way it's been," we seem to say, "and this is the way it will remain."

Maybe we need adversity to grab our attention to force us to walk down a new path or go in a different direction. Again, in principle, I know this is true.

I don't want to imply that if things are going well, we're getting set up for chaos. I do believe, however, that when life gets too comfortable, we become content and lose our spiritual edge.

The difference is an awareness of the source of our good life. As long as we continue to remind ourselves of God's gracious provision and daily outpouring of love, we can avoid self-satisfaction.

Complacency reminds me of an example regarding our son. We had lived in Kenya, East Africa, for two years before an Asian friend invited our family into Masai territory in the Rift Valley. All three of our children had been immensely excited, especially our then four-year-old, John Mark. The animals roamed freely across the landscape. Our Asian friend took us in his truck, and we loved zooming over the flat plains and seeing the abundance of wild game.

John Mark loved counting them, and he kept a running total in his head of the number of zebras, wildebeests, giraffes, elephants and all of the others. It seemed as if he couldn't see enough.

By noon of the second day our son stopped counting. "There! See the ostrich!" I pointed. "See! Over there are three elephants!"

He didn't bother to look, so I asked, "What's wrong?"

"There's nothing but animals," he said.

We laughed, but it made us realize how easily we adjust to situations, that we can soon learn to take for granted even the most exotic locations or an abundance of wealth.

I thought of that concept of complacency during the time of God's hidden face. This became even more significant when I read, "I was carefree and thought, 'I'll never be shaken!' You, LORD, were my friend, and you made me strong as a mighty mountain. But when you hid your face, I was crushed" (Ps. 30:6-7, *CEV*).

The psalm writer spoke of his own complacency. Apparently things were going well for him and then something must have happened, because he says, "When you hid your face, I was crushed."

As I thought of those words, I felt a strong sense of identity with the poet. I considered the months before the onset of the starless night. Life had gone well for me and, in retrospect, I had become spiritually careless. I had lost my spiritual edge.

I saw this work in two parts of my life—personally and professionally. It's easier to talk about the professional, so I'll do that first.

I was a full-time freelance writer. For 15 years I had worked hard to make a living at the profession, and it had happened. The first half-dozen years I must have prayed every day for God to provide enough contracts for me to earn a living. Over the years I'd begun to feel an assurance of God's provision.

That part was good and enabled me to trust and relax. My role was to do my job and leave finances to God. During the next couple of years I had begun to take my lifestyle for granted. God was in charge; everything would work out.

At no time during the period when God turned off the lights did financial survival become an issue. In fact, my income increased. Our standard of living went up and, at one point, I started to get careless with the way I spent money.

It wasn't an issue about money, but it was the encroaching darkness that surrounded me, and with it the confusion and the lack of God's presence. That's what troubled me. It was as if God had been around, and I assumed He would always be around. Then He turned off the lights and disappeared.

As I examined my life, I admitted that I had been careless in spending. Not that I had done anything wrong. It was merely that I had lost that sense of dependence on God's provision for me. I realized that God could close doors as easily as open them.

Standards of Consistency

The second part was personal and much more difficult to cope with. I had been a Christian long enough to have developed a theological lifestyle. That is, my wife and I tried to live the kind of lives that we felt honored God.

The problem I had to face was the temptation not to impose that lifestyle on others. I'll list two examples of our lifestyle. First, Shirley and I never missed church service. If we had guests, they stayed home or went with us. Second, we made a financial commitment to God and, no matter how difficult our finances, we always took God's portion off the top.

I began to see that some of the people in the church—and often they were the elders and leaders—didn't live what I called "consistently." It took me a long time to figure out that when we're complacent about our own relationship, we tend then to look judgmentally at others. That was a hard reality to face, but again

I could hear the words of Nathan: "You are the man!"

After a lengthy period of darkness, and walking with a shamed face, I admitted to myself that I had looked down on those who weren't living faithfully (as I defined the word). How could that man be an elder when he only comes to church about twice a month? How could she teach a women's study group when she admitted that she opened the leader's guidebook only half an hour before the class began? I had other little ways in which I compared myself to other people.

I didn't say it out loud, and to do so would have exposed my self-righteous attitude: Who commanded Cec Murphey to check out everyone's spiritual barometer? When did God give me the right to set the standards of behavior?

For several days I struggled over my complacent-turned-judgmental attitude. I read the words from James: "Brothers and sisters, do not slander one another. Anyone who speaks against a brother or sister or judges them speaks against the law and judges it. When you judge the law, you are not keeping it, but sitting in judgment on it. There is only one Lawgiver and Judge. . . . But you—who are you to judge your neighbor?" (Jas. 4:11-12).

I also thought of the strong admonition by Paul, who took the Romans to task for criticizing each other. "What right do you have to criticize someone else's servants? Only their Lord can decide if they are doing right, and the Lord will make sure that they do right" (Rom. 14:4, CEV).

In those days of silence, the Holy Spirit forced me to face my attitude. The biggest part of the battle for me was to admit to myself that I felt so harsh or judgmental about what constituted righteous living. Somewhere during those days and nights—

because even the day seemed like night—I heard myself pray, "God, I'm like the Pharisee who boasted in prayer in the Temple, 'God, I thank you that I am not like other people—robbers, evildoers, adulterers—or even like this tax collector. I fast twice a week and give a tenth of all I get'" (Luke 18:11-12).

Was that a picture of me? "Surely not," I said.

But a quiet inner voice taunted, "Yes, it is you."

At first I had protested in silence. *That doesn't sound like me.*

"Oh?" I heard a deeper, inner part of me ask.

"That's me on the page," I admitted.

That startling revelation filled me with shame. In those days, when I encountered those painful moments, I liked to walk to the wooded area near our house—to stroll the trails that wind over several acres. Something about the leaves under my feet, the soft birdcalls, the occasional scampering of a squirrel and the isolation from others enabled me to think more clearly.

During that period of time, I printed out several Bible verses on three-by-five-inch index cards and read them as I walked. Here is one of them: "'I'll never be shaken!' You, LORD, were my friend, and you made me strong as a mighty mountain. But when you hid your face, I was crushed" (Ps. 30:6-7, *CEV*).

I couldn't get away from the last sentence: "But when you hid your face, I was crushed." Although it had been my own self-righteousness that caused me to feel ashamed, I realized God wanted me to grasp the power of that verse.

I focused on the word "crushed," which fit my mood. Other translators opted for words such as "troubled" or "dismayed," but they seemed weak. The next verses in Psalm 30 show how God's hidden face had an impact on the psalmist. He goes on to say that he prayed and asked, "What good will it do you if I am in the grave? . . . How can I praise you or tell how loyal you are? Have pity, LORD! Help!" (Ps. 30:9-10, *CEV*).

It amazed me that immediately the poet finishes the psalm with words about turning sorrow into joyful dancing. In fact, that was becoming a pattern in my reading of the psalms. The writer wails from the pit of despair and at the end of his lament, he is able to praise God. I wished I knew what had gone on between the writing of "Help!" in verse 10 to the note of joy in verse 11.

Frustration tugged at me because I kept encountering that jump in psalm after psalm. And then I thought, *Perhaps it's a natural flow—not a long, reflective pause between verses.* Is it possible that by freely admitting the pain and hardship, that acknowledgment— the realization—began the healing process?

Is it possible that the moments when the psalmist felt the most crushed were exactly the moments when he realized that God's face was no longer hidden? When he was on top of things and living in satisfied smugness, God turned off the lights. Now that he was low and despairing, perhaps that's when God began to smile on him once again.

The last two verses abound with effusive praise: "You have turned my sorrow into joyful dancing. No longer am I sad and wearing sackcloth. I thank you from my heart, and I will never stop singing your praises, my LORD and my God" (Ps. 30:11-12, *CEV*).

Whatever happened at least brought him out of complacency and made him view God with joyousness.

I hadn't reached that place, but I knew that's what I wanted. I was still living in verse 7, where God hid His face, and feeling cast off by God. I wanted to rush ahead to the end of the psalm and read the words of praise.

But it wasn't ready to happen yet.

I heard myself ask, as I had been asking for months, *How long, O Lord? How long?* I had no answer, but I sensed I was getting closer to the dawn.

—⁓—

When the dawn broke through,
so would joy. I waited.

10

AFFLICTIVE
PROVIDENCES

Years ago, when I was reading one of the English Puritans, I stumbled over the statement that went something like this: "Afflictive providences are of great value to the people of God."

When the writer used the term "providence," he referred to an accepted theological concept that isn't spelled out in the Bible, but the effect is there. Briefly, providence is God's working with His people to fulfill His divine purpose in their lives. If we focus on the idea of God *providing,* we stay close to the meaning. It is the continuous activity within creation by which God preserves and governs the world.

Providence implies that God's absolute rule includes all creation and denies that chance or fate governs the universe. Providence means the provision and protection of those who follow the Lord. God acts in accordance with the laws and principles established in the world in the beginning.

The Puritan I read made a case that we *need* "afflicted providence," or, I would say, we need to struggle with God's hidden face. We can back this up with a number of verses such as Romans 8:35: "Who shall separate us from the love of Christ? Shall trouble or hardship or persecution or famine or nakedness or danger or sword?"

Paul's question is rhetorical, and its words promise that nothing can make a permanent division between believers and Jesus

Christ. But it also implies that we will face such things. In fact, some of Paul's readers may already have experienced the trouble, suffering and hard times to which he referred.

Afflictive providence turns up all through the Bible. One of my favorite biblical examples is Joseph. Jacob's favorite son may have been a nasty kid, but he didn't deserve to be sold as a slave or flung into prison for a crime he didn't commit. Yet Joseph triumphed and ended up preserving the life of his entire family (see Gen. 37–47).

We can't bypass Job's story. At one time nothing but problems and troubles held him tight. He couldn't talk about his lands or reputation, health or family because they were all gone. He only could cry out and say, "I know that my redeemer lives" (Job 19:25).

Obviously, I couldn't compare my external circumstances to Joseph's or Job's. I did find some comfort in my confusion and pain by thinking how well they handled their afflictive providences.

During the period when God had the lights turned off, I knew He would hit the light switch again, but that didn't make the situation less painful. My faith reminded me of God's promises and faithfulness. I read of Paul's struggles, and he said, "We never give up. Our bodies are gradually dying, but we ourselves are being made stronger each day. These little troubles are getting us ready for an eternal glory that will make all our troubles seem like nothing. Things that are seen don't last forever" (2 Cor. 4:16-18a, CEV). Intellectually, I knew that as well.

What I didn't like to acknowledge was my need for the afflictive providences. If I have understood the Puritans' writings properly, they weren't simply saying that we'd have to confront afflictions and problems, or that hardships would come. The term means that we *need* them—that they're part of God's providential care for us. That is, afflictive providences are necessary for our growth. If I believe them, it meant that God decided I had to walk around in the starless night for my good. Again, on some intellectual plane, I assented to that statement. Emotionally, I couldn't quite accept such a concept.

God's Plan

Yet I did realize God planned for my period of darkness. To make it meaningful, I had to say it even stronger: The Spirit led me, pushed me or kicked me into darkness. The sunless side of God's face didn't slip up on me. It was part of God's loving care for me. It didn't feel very loving.

I did think about an incident in the life of Jesus. In Matthew 3 is the story of Jesus' baptism by John the Baptist. Afterward, the heavens opened and God said, "This is my Son, whom I love; with him I am well pleased" (3:17). The very next statement, separated by a chapter break, says that the Spirit drove Jesus into the wilderness to be tempted by the devil (see 4:1). After 40 days of testing, Jesus began His public ministry.

That certainly came under the heading of afflictive providences. The problem I faced is that I'm not Jesus. I didn't see any great public ministry staring at me. I saw nothing but blackness and emptiness ahead. Right then I wanted only to walk in the light once again.

During those months, I had entered into afflictive providences. God put me through the tests by shutting out the lights and making things difficult for me. I kept thinking, *If only I could feel God or have some evidence of God at work in my life.* At one of the worst points, numbness became my constant companion. I felt nothing. I wasn't angry, sad, joyous or anxious. I felt as if my emotions had been stored in the deep freeze. I simply didn't feel anything.

I read my Bible; I claimed Bible promises; I made spiritual commitments, but those were acts of the will and didn't come from feelings of spiritual hunger or even acts of desperation.

One night, I got out of bed and went into our living room, where I stayed on my knees. I decided I'd pray until I forced my way through to God. I might as well have gone to sleep. I don't know how long I prayed, but in the middle of the night, I realized my spiritual temperature hovered in the subfreezing range, as it had before I started to pray. I gave up and went to bed.

The saints of old would probably have counseled by saying, "Providence may truly delay the performance of those mercies for which you have waited and prayed. Wait, for God will answer."

I was tired of waiting.

What's the Difference?

I had come to the place where it didn't seem to make much difference. I walked in that place where I felt afflicted, but I didn't care if it was God, the devil or my own doing. I know only that, as far as I was concerned, my spiritual tank registered empty.

During one of those extremely dark nights, I read Psalm 102, which begins: "Hear my prayer, LORD; let my cry for help come to you. Do not hide your face from me when I am in distress. Turn your ear to me; when I call, answer me quickly" (Ps. 102:1-2).

I read, and as I continued further into the psalm, I became aware that his words don't get any better. He was sinking low, and he presents about the worst picture any believer can describe. In fact, the psalm's title is "A prayer of an afflicted person who has grown weak and pours out a lament before the LORD." Those words of the title—inspired or not—sum up the statements rather well.

As I read Psalm 102, besides the opening verses that speak of God's hidden face, the place where I resonated most was in verse 7: "I lie awake; I have become like a bird alone on a roof." In his affliction, he felt absolutely alone. He had nowhere to turn or no one to listen to him.

During my bleak period, one Saturday morning, squawking noises filled the air and I could hear wings flapping. When I looked out the window, a flock of starlings had invaded my front yard. Hundreds of them descended like a black cloud. I'd seen them before, and they came around two or three times a year. Then I realized I had never seen only one starling pecking away; the large group always flocked together.

The fact that I even thought about a lone bird shows a picture of my spiritual and emotional state. In the midst of the many I thought of the one—and compared it to me.

I wasn't a lone bird. I had friends who would have consoled me if I contacted them, but I couldn't call. Even if they called me, I couldn't have said, "I need your listening ear and understanding heart." I felt too confused to talk. I would have to try to explain the unexplainable for anyone to understand, and I didn't know if I could make clear what I was going through.

I tried to comfort myself by looking around me. I saw homeless people and the terminally ill, families unable to pay their rent or utilities. Yet I was so focused on my problems and me, it was a time when I couldn't concentrate on the needs of others.

The writer of the psalm catalogued the complaints and said, "For I eat ashes as my food and mingle my drink with tears because of your great wrath, for you have taken me up and thrown me aside" (102:9-10).

I can see two ways to interpret his statement about God's wrath (or some translate it as *indignation*). It can be a blaming complaint, as if the writer says, "God, I tried to do everything right, but You got mad at me." I've felt that way at times. One translation reads, "Because you are furious and have thrown me aside" (*CEV*).

Or, more likely, and the position I think is correct, is that the writer had a sense of justice. It's a cry for help, but it's also an acknowledgment that says, "I deserve everything I've gotten. You put up with me long enough. You sent your people to warn me, to counsel me, to plead with me, but I didn't listen. Finally, I pushed you to the line where you said, 'No more. This is the end.'"

When he writes, "For you have taken me up and thrown me aside" (v. 10), I hear that as his saying, "I've been cursed by people and cast away by God."

What does that mean to suffer the indignation or the fury of God? I meant that as a question by me, a professing Christian. Was that indeed what I was going through?

Feeling Alone

Yes, I understood that unknown poet in Babylon. He may have been in some kind of environment where thousands of people milled around him, but his wasn't a state of physical aloneness but of emotional isolation. Yes, I understood that feeling because that's the same circuitous, winding trail I was hiking along. One of the worst parts of my journey was the feeling that no one could understand where I was.

Regardless of how I labeled it, the sense of utter aloneness seemed too private to talk about and too pervasive to ignore. Even if I had wanted to talk, I couldn't find how to express the stage of the journey I was going through.

I came up with several analogies, such as being a tiny ship on a huge ocean with no navigational equipment. As I examined my life and tried to talk about it, I thought of my years of working in what was called the men's movement—a secular movement that began in the mid-1980s.

We men gathered, sometimes hundreds of us. We openly dealt with issues such as learning to feel and express our emotions, sexual and physical abuse, relating to our wives and learning to trust other men. Steve Grubman-Black, who became a close friend, once said, "I feel as if I'm journeying through a wilderness where no one has ever been before. I don't have a marked trail, so I have no idea where I'm going to end up."

I understood Steve's isolation and confusion. His journey differed from mine, but we reached out toward each other. We wanted someone—even one person—to intuit what we felt.

Someone in the men's movement gave me a copy of one of Edgar Allan Poe's lesser-known poems called "Alone." Strangely enough I had read it at an earlier time when I was searching for God in my life. That too had been a lonely, isolated time.

—⁓—

From childhood's hour I have not been
As others were—I have not seen
As others saw—I could not bring
My passions from a common spring . . .
And all I lov'd, I lov'd alone.

—⁓—

Alone. Yes, I understood. So did a number of the men who read it. It struck the right note for those of us in our afflictive providences.

Little Things

I had failed God in many little ways. I did things I knew were wrong—not grossly wrong—but little things through neglect or an attitude that says, "It doesn't really matter."

Examining those little things made me extremely uncomfortable. I turned to the New Testament, thinking that I'd read more about grace and could ease up on my diet of guilt and shame. I kept reminding myself that it wasn't fair for me to compare my situation with those exiles. Whenever I did that—and I did it often—it simply made me feel more alone and afflicted.

I realized that I hadn't suffered physically, but I understood the emotional tone of the psalm. I hadn't undergone privation, loss of citizenship, destruction of everything I owned or the death of those close to me. Yet I identified with the psalm. *What if I am suffering the indignation or wrath of God?* I asked. What if I have done hundreds, even thousands, of tiny acts of disobedience? What if God now says, "You have reached the end, and you'll go no farther"? Was that what was going on? Could it be that God's hidden face came because of my failures?

The more I thought of that, the more I realized something. If that were true, even the indignation of God had a therapeutic purpose. God didn't show fury just to show fury or because of a lack of self-control.

And yet I said to myself, *Suppose there is a grand purpose in this. Suppose God is making me feel like the lonely bird on the roof so that something will happen to change me. What if this isn't about sin or disobedience? What if this is about God's grace at work in my life?*

The more I contemplated this, the more I realized that if I have any understanding of the Bible, it's that God's anger toward the covenant people was to turn them around and call them back into fellowship. Perhaps this was my needed afflicted providence.

At that time, I was still so caught up in my sense of isolation that I didn't react to my own words, and yet I knew they were right. Over the next few days, as I continued to reread Psalm 102, I saw the principle clearly. The words of verse 17 are: "He will respond to the prayer of the destitute; he will not despise their plea."

That provided a slim note of hope for me. I wasn't able to shout and dance, but deep, deep inside, a tiny voice whispered, "Yes."

God wouldn't throw me away forever. It had only felt that way. And I realized afresh the power of my own feelings of emptiness. It was one more time when I had to remind myself of God's loving faithfulness, no matter how my emotions had numbed out.

Common sense says it's a perception rather than reality and at a low period of life. It's like saying, "No one else in the world knows exactly what I'm feeling." It doesn't matter whether others can feel our desolation. When we're going through the pain, we don't care if they do or don't. Our pain is our own. It's as if we need to suffer ourselves, in isolation, and feel the depth of our despair. We may go for help especially when the emotion persists or we can't drag ourselves out of the deep pit, but initially at least, it's private pain. It's an arctic bitter coldness we can't share with another human being.

Restoration Will Come

One Sunday morning, I sat in church, not fully attuned to what was going on that day. I opened my Bible to follow a passage in 1 Peter that our pastor, David Fry, would use in his sermon. One verse grabbed my attention: "And the God of all grace, who called you to his eternal glory in Christ, after you have suffered a little while, will himself restore you and make you strong, firm and steadfast" (1 Pet. 5:10).

That was a word from God to me—the first direct word I'd heard from God in nearly 18 months. It felt as if God had sent a ray of light from heaven that touched the numbness of my heart that morning.

"After you have suffered a little," I repeated quietly to myself. Those words brought me immense comfort, although I don't think I heard much of the sermon that morning.

It was one of those times when I felt God touch me lightly and whisper, "Listen." I didn't have a powerful, overwhelming experience, and it was actually quiet, but it stayed with me all day. I sensed God meant that in the divine plan, after I have suffered enough, things would change.

Only now, as I look back over that dark period of my life, can I honestly say that I needed the afflictive providences. I needed the turmoil, the hardship and the emotional pain. I needed them because I had committed myself to grow as a believer in Jesus Christ. God never said I had to enjoy affliction, but maybe it's enough for me to understand that I needed the loving, afflictive providence of a caring God.

I also found comfort when I thought of the statement about Jesus in Hebrews 5:8: "Son though he was, he learned obedience from what he suffered." There are some lessons in life that we learn only the hard way—through the path of pain.

Most Christians acknowledge that hardships and difficulties make our character stronger and mature our faith. That year and a half of darkness was a difficult, discouraging period in my life. I hated going through those times. Yet in all the honesty I can muster, I have to say, I wouldn't give up those experiences for anything. I also have to say, I don't ever want to have to repeat them.

"It hurts too much," I've told God. But I sense that God only smiles at my words. God knows, and I know that I'll have those periods again. When it happens again, maybe the next time I'll have learned enough to smile and rise above them. But I doubt I'll be able to do that. However, I can also say that each time I've encountered the absence of God's face, I'm a little stronger in the battle. That is, I seem to be less discouraged in the midst of the darkness. That doesn't make it easy. I can't speak for anyone else, especially for the great saints of the faith, but I can tell you that even when I have some understanding about what's going on, it still hurts.

—⁓—

That's the idea behind afflictive providence—it hurts because
it's meant to hurt. But it's also God's loving, compassionate
way to direct us down the right paths.

11

SECRET SINS

All of us know about secret sins, especially when they become public. The married evangelist has a liaison with a single woman, and she tells the sordid details to the media; the highly respected banker absconds with funds; the closet homosexual is diagnosed with AIDS. Few of those stories shock us because we know about such things. They're secret sins, hidden from the world but never from God.

We hear about them virtually every week from the newspapers, the Internet or TV news. They're the terrible deeds done in secret by people—usually known throughout the community as the good people, or in the church as the committed Christians. They're done under what we call "the cover of darkness" because they don't want anyone else to know, and they don't want to get caught.

That concept lines up with Psalm 90:8, in which the writer addresses God: "You have set our iniquities before you, our secret sins in the light of your presence." The obvious interpretation of that verse is that God not only knows our secret sins but also spotlights them for the whole world to know.

That may be the right interpretation, but I wonder.

I think of another verse about secret sins: "Who can understand *his* errors? Cleanse me from secret *faults*. Keep back Your servant also from presumptuous *sins*; let them not have dominion over me" (Ps. 19:12-13, *NKJV*, emphasis added).

That was from pre-Christian writings, and one commentator refers to the secret faults as "sins of inadvertence" that God's people could deal with by the sacrificial system outlined in Leviticus.

That may be the right interpretation, but I wonder.

Since the times when I have walked in the darkness, I've begun to think of secret sins differently. It may be that I'm looking at the topic too subjectively and missing some of the objectivity of it. Still, it has a ring of truth to me.

Here's how I see it. First, our secret sins *are* sins. The Bible makes that clear. But the significant fact is that they are secret. *In fact, I think they are so secret that they are kept hidden from us, the perpetrators.*

Read again the words of Psalm 19:12 as the writer prays, "Who can understand *his* errors? Cleanse me from secret *faults*." Who else but a conscientious, committed believer would dare to pray such a request? Isn't that indicative of a burning desire—even a yearning—to know the truth about himself?

Isn't it possible that the psalmist could be asking, "God, show me the sins I commit that I don't even recognize, the kind of sins that would horrify me if I faced them. Help me see what I'm doing that I'm blind to"?

Isn't it possible that the words of Psalm 90:8 might have the same idea in mind: "You have set our iniquities before you, our secret sins in the light of your presence"? Is it possible that our iniquities become known to us *only* because of "the light of" God's presence?

Self-Deception

As I read such statements, I acknowledge there are secret sins. Our blindness is what makes them secret. Or here's another way to frame it: we have developed such a capacity for denial and self-delusion that we keep ourselves from seeing what we don't want to acknowledge.

When I think of self-deception, my first reaction is to remember a woman named Edna Mae Baldwin. Back in the neighborhood where I lived as a kid, Mrs. Baldwin had a son a year older than I was, named Kenneth. He was a bright, good-looking boy. And a first-class sneak. Among other things, he used to steal candy bars from the neighborhood grocery store and brag about it. One time, the grocer, Mr. Neugerbauer, caught him and took him to Mrs. Baldwin. I was there with Kenneth's younger brother and heard everything.

She yelled at Mr. Neugerbauer, cursed him and told him he was not only mistaken but was also lying. "My son does not steal. We have money for candy any time he wants it."

Even then—and I must have been about 12 years old—I didn't think she was lying. Many times I had heard her talk to my mother and to others about Kenneth, who was her special son. She believed he was a nice, well-mannered boy. I don't know why, but I wondered if it was because that's what she wanted to believe or if she couldn't accept that her son was less than perfect. I do know that no one could convince her that he was bad.

Another time, the police came to her house and found hidden in her backyard a pair of shoes that Kenneth had stolen. "One of those Marlin kids put them there," she shouted at the police. "Those are the kids you need to arrest. My Kenneth does not steal."

No one pressed charges as I recall, but that mother never saw any wrongdoing in her son. (They moved a year or so later to another part of the state. I don't know if she ever learned the truth about Kenneth.)

That's the power of self-delusion. It's also the way of secret sins in our life. As observers, however, it's easy enough to see others' faults of unawareness. Here's a recent one. I've been working with a newer writer that I'll call Rich. He's one of those people for whom the term "self-absorbed" must have been invented. When he calls and I'm not home, my wife says, he sulks because I'm not available to help him.

One day, he wanted to talk to me, but I had had a death in the family and said, "I don't feel like talking today." He said he understood. The next day he phoned me twice about something he was writing. He didn't ask about my grief, the circumstances about my relative's death or even how I felt.

Yet I know Rich well enough that he considers himself a warm, caring person. He can be—and often is—quite charming; yet I'm sure he has no awareness of his own self-absorption.

As an outsider, that's my viewpoint. If I'm seeing the situation correctly, I would say that self-absorption is one of Rich's secret sins.

I'm not immune to secret sins. Facing that aspect of my life may be one of the largest aspects of my own growth in recent months. I've begun to stare at my own secret sins. Some days I feel as if the spotlight of God's presence has focused on those things. And I feel awful.

The circumstances that led me down that path of self-discovery aren't important, but I want to point out what happened after God opened my eyes. My first response, of course, was absolute and categorical denial. I couldn't believe that I was guilty. For a couple of days after my initial awareness, I refused to consider it. When I finally faced what I needed to see, it was as if I looked into a mirror with a thousand-watt light behind it. Every blemish and line showed. I recoiled at what I saw. A revolting sense of shame raced through me.

That's me? I shuddered at the thought.

As I pondered what I had seen, I must have been in a state of shock. *Is that me?* I asked myself again and again. No matter how I tried to deny it, I knew the answer.

My experience made me think of Adam and Eve in the garden, and I had an inkling of identity with their shame. They had walked around for a long time, totally naked. Once they sinned—and the Bible says their eyes were opened—they knew their nakedness (see Gen. 3:10). For the first time they knew what had always been, yet they had had no awareness of not having on clothes. When they knew, they felt ashamed. The only way they knew how to hide their nakedness—and their vulnerability—was to make clothes out of leaves and jump behind the bushes when God came along.

I had read their story before. I'd never identified with it. But now that God's silence pushed me into looking at my backside, I saw things I didn't want to see. Yet that's what we come up against when we struggle to find our way out of the darkness. We cry out, "Help me learn. Show me what I need to see."

God answers our prayer, but we don't want that kind of answer. It comes in such a way that we can't admit or believe it is God at work. Where are the tender mercies of God? Where is the manifestation of loving-kindness? We get hit with shame and deep inner pain. Instead of affirmation and praise, God shines the spotlight on our nakedness. And like our original parents, we feel thoroughly shamed.

When that happened to me, I covered myself with a heavy cloak of depression. For three days, I walked around and did my work mechanically. My mind refused to turn away from what I had seen. *If the things I glimpsed were true, how could I live with myself?* I asked. What if others saw my secret shame and I didn't? I felt even worse as I asked, *Do people actually know those terrible things about me that I haven't known myself?* I knew the answer was yes.

Now that I've explained my reaction to seeing my secret sin, I'm going to get more specific.

During the period when I had to live under the divine eclipse, I had searched my heart and yearned for a clearer reflection of my inner self. I even sang the old hymn about "nothing between my soul and the Savior, so that His blessed face may be seen."

Shameful Pride

For a long time, I'd carried around a particular image of myself, which is that I'm a committed Christian, a rather nice person who cares about other people, and someone who likes to help others. In fact, I do care, and I'm willing to go out of my way to help. Someone has called me a cheerleader for others, and I like hearing words like that. I've mentored a number of people, especially other writers. One of my protégées, Gloria Spencer, said, "Cec does some writing to support his mentoring."

How do you think I felt when I heard Gloria say those words? *Proud* correctly answers it.

Did I acknowledge the pride I felt? Of course not. I deflected the compliment, brushed it away and even laughed at such a thing. But inwardly—*secretly*—I glowed with pride.

That wasn't easy to confess, especially on paper. It's difficult because pride is one thing I've never associated with myself. My friends have called me kind, gentle, warm and caring. Folks who don't like me have called me stubborn, angry and mean. But *no one*—to my knowledge—ever called me proud.

From my earliest Christian experiences, I had heard that pride was the cardinal sin. My teachers said that was what made Satan a fallen angel.

No one ever called me proud. That is, no one until a Sunday evening in October. It was such a painful experience that I wrote it in my journal, and I remember it well.

A few days earlier, through my reading, the word "proud" had hit me, but I laughed and thought, *Not me.*

That Sunday, however, God pointed a finger that accompanied the divine searchlight. I didn't like it, didn't want to hear it, couldn't accept it and didn't believe it came from God anyway. I had developed my self-deception skills so well that I couldn't hear such words.

The following morning, I went for a long walk in the woods near my house, and I prayed. I felt such a mass of turmoil inside myself. I hadn't been hearing God answer my calls, but at least I hadn't heard static on the line. Then I began to pray for God to show me the truth about myself. I pleaded with God to show me who I am.

That was a dangerous thing to ask.

Like a shock to my brain, I heard the word "pride" from deep within myself. I paused near a red oak and looked upward. *This can't be true.* I started to walk on.

Somewhere between a black oak and a native dogwood, the tears came. I felt the way I imagined King David must have responded when Nathan the prophet accused him of committing adultery with Bathsheba. Nathan pointed his finger and said, "You are the man!" (2 Sam. 12:7, *NKJV*). He went on to say, "Why have you despised the commandment of the LORD, to do evil in His sight?" (v. 9, *NKJV*).

A thundering silence from within cut more deeply than 25 well-meaning people could have done by accusing me.

God had answered. I couldn't escape. Yes, I was the man, and I saw my secret sin and cringed in horror. "God, I've been blinded to my shortcomings," I yelled out. Almost immediately I heard myself say, "No, it's more than shortcomings. It's my secret sin."

For several hours, the shame remained intense. It took two more days before I fully worked through it. During that time, I asked myself again and again, *What makes this so shameful? What is it about facing the reality of pride that tortures me in ways other sins don't?*

The following week, I was able to talk to my closest confidant, David Morgan. He hugged me and talked to me in a way that made me know he understood. He said something like this: "You have this image of yourself. It's not who you are. It's more like some ideal self you keep trying to live up to. And you've encased the image in a suit of protective armor. Whenever something happens to break through that armor, you feel deflated. The deflation hurts. To get over this, you have to face that you're not who you have idealized yourself to be."

Of all the things I have gone through during the time of God's hidden face, that has been the hardest for me to face. I wanted to know the truth about myself, but I didn't want it to hurt.

The end of this episode is that I did find peace.

I was walking after dark on October 22. I had hit a low point. I remember feeling as Cain did when God pronounced a curse on him. "My punishment is more than I can bear" (Gen. 4:13). Like Cain, a heavy weight descended on me that I didn't feel I could hold up under.

I started back home with my head bent low. I didn't want to see or talk to anyone. I wished I could turn invisible. Half a block from my house a new thought came to me. I heard my own voice say, "God, You already know all this about me. You've known it all along. You've seen my pride and all the other secret sins. *And You've loved me anyway.*"

—⋙—

The shame lifted. A quiet peace came over me,
and then joyousness. It was going to be all right.
The inflicted pain was part of the healing.

12

OLD WOUNDS

"All of us have four or five core issues in life," David Morgan said. He's a therapist and my closest friend. "And we spend most of our lives exploring them." He went on to say that we deal with an issue and "resolve" it and feel it's taken care of, "but it keeps coming back on some other level." David talked about our core issues being on a cone-shaped spiral. The spiral keeps turning, and we deal with one of those core issues at another place on the spiral.

He pointed out that those core issues are formed during our childhood and that we never fully recover. He didn't say it, but I thought of it as being somewhat like some forms of addiction. We win over the problem, and we may never yield to it again, yet it's always there, constantly trying to sneak back into our life.

That concept helps me see that growing in faith means not only struggling with those basic issues, but it reminds me that those issues remain an ongoing battle—and require vigilance to win over them. The dead issues don't remain dead; they resurrect themselves and transmute into other forms, but they're still there.

Abandonment

I once had a friend who had a terrible childhood. (For his protection, I'll call him Tim.) His parents physically abandoned him when he was young. They dropped him off at a relative's house and asked if they'd take care of him for "a couple of days." They left, and it was more than three years before he saw either of them again.

I have no idea why they did that to Tim, and he never chose to try to explain. But his sharing that part of his life enabled me to understand how core issues continue to influence behavior and crop up in the way we strive to have our needs met.

Through years of counseling and two wrecked marriages, Tim said he had finally resolved his abandonment issues. But I observed one thing about him—the importance of money. When the stock market went down, he felt depressed. More than once he spoke of his fear of becoming homeless and alone.

At first glance that behavior or that fear may not sound like childhood abandonment. I'm convinced it was, except that it had appeared at a different place on the spiral. The emotional and physical abandonment had twisted itself into financial cravings. Tim seemed to view everything through dollar signs. He wasn't outwardly stingy or greedy, but it didn't take long in our friendship for me to realize that money controlled his life, and Tim never seemed aware of that fact.

"Money means nothing to me," he said. I don't think he was lying; I think he was unaware of the pull of finances on his life. Or he'd say, "I'm a practical man. I like to know the cost of things."

The last time I saw Tim, he was three years away from taking an early retirement from his company. He hated his job, and he detested walking through the doors every morning. "Why don't you quit?" I asked. "You can get another job." He had the marketable skills and education to do that easily enough. But he had been with the company 17 years.

"If I hang on for 20, I'll almost double my retirement benefits."

I didn't answer, and I'm not trying to play therapist. But if I had said to him, "You're afraid to quit because money means security to you," he would have argued with me. One time I did try to tie it to his abandonment as a child, and he shook his head. "I handled that years ago. It's no longer an issue."

As I watched Tim over 17 years of friendship, I saw the same problems come up and manifest themselves in other forms.

Although Tim's problems may seem obvious, I think that's the way we humans live. The form of the temptations change, and, because of God's help, sometimes they become less powerful. They don't totally disappear.

Temper

One more illustration. I have a friend who once had a violent temper. As a teen, he almost killed another boy in a rage over a trivial issue—trivial in that it aroused his anger, but it was an anger that changed my friend. When he realized what he had done, he was horrified at his actions and prayed for God to forgive him and take away his temper. It was a long, painful ordeal, but he says that in the 30 years since, he has never been angry with anyone and that he owes that victory all to God.

I don't want to hurt his self-image, but he's a grudge carrier. If someone hurts his feelings, he doesn't yell, beat him with his fists or show any negative emotion. He holds it inside. He won't speak badly about those offending people—in fact, he erases them out of his life.

I know that's true because, inadvertently, I hurt his feelings. Later, I wrote and apologized. We had been good friends, and yet it's now been nearly a decade since I wrote to him. He's never contacted me or acknowledged my apology. I doubt that he ever will.

For a long time I didn't understand how our issues—our old wounds—affect us all through our life. It became extremely apparent to me when I went through my dark, dark night.

After I had fallen deeply into the pit of darkness, I assumed that it wouldn't be a long time period. My two previous walks in the starless nights had taught me many lessons. The first time I had wandered in inky space for about seven months, and the second time it had lasted only a few weeks. I had grown through the years, so I assumed this experience would lead to a quick ascent, perhaps even an easy upward climb. After all, previously I had been down there at that bottom a long time. I had learned much from the experiences. Wasn't it time to graduate to a new level of spirituality? In my naiveté I must have harbored some kind of illusion that I'd surge forward unhindered by problems and live in triumph. I had learned; I had overcome; I was a victor.

Then, in the middle of that darkness (although, of course, I didn't know it was the middle), I became aware of my old wounds and how they crept in and deceived me.

After that, I committed myself to pray every day these words: "God, strip away my self-delusions and give me the grace to accept the truth about myself."

Looking back, I think it was a radical way to pray, and had I realized the emotional consequences, I probably would have been too cowardly to ask God to do that. This had come about, as I've mentioned in my chapter called "Secret Sins," with my awareness of what I called my ideal self. That was the way I wanted others to see me, the way I wanted to see myself; and it was the way I honestly believed I was.

Self-Delusions

When I prayed for God to strip away my self-delusions, I had no idea what I asked. One of those realizations came through an experience I'll simply call a time of rejection. And in trying to cope,

I came to realize that it was an old wound, something that sneaked up on me in several forms.

Someone had rejected me—intuitively I had known it was coming—and I had also realized that a part of me wanted it to happen. Eventually, I realized that I had wanted that person out of my life anyway and didn't have what it took to take the initiative. He angrily rejected me by slamming the door, sealing it and putting a lock on it.

I went into a depressive mode for a couple of hours. That evening, when I rode to a meeting with a friend, I felt only slightly better, and I told him about the incident.

"Then why are you upset?" he asked.

"What?" I asked, hardly able to believe that he didn't understand.

"You don't want a relationship with him, you expected the break and he cut you off. I'd think that would settle everything."

"Rejection," I said. "It hurts to be rejected."

My friend didn't say another word. After several minutes of silence between us, one of us began to talk on a different topic.

How did I feel when my friend confronted me with, "Why are you upset?" Frankly, I felt a little worse. *I tried to explain to a friend and he couldn't understand or maybe didn't even care about my pain.*

The next day I thought about that scene in the car. My friend, although not very sensitive to me and my need, was actually right to raise the question. I can't read his mind, of course, but I think he assumed I would work through it, and he didn't seem to think the situation was a big deal.

Ah, that's the point, I thought. *It isn't that big an issue.* My relationship with the other person had been deteriorating for months. The ending was inevitable. Yet when it came, I fell apart.

What's going on? I asked myself.

I had read somewhere that when we overreact to a situation, we're actually reacting to something else. I thought about that quite a bit, and truth slowly slipped into my consciousness.

"Rejection" *was* the significant word. What that former friend had done only triggered a reaction to something that reached back into my past. After much heart searching I thought of the pain labeled *rejection* that had come through my life, from my earliest days of childhood. My sense at that moment was that it had hurt deeply. Instead of allowing myself to feel that early childhood pain and stay with it until healing came, I had locked it into a vault.

Every once in a while, new rejections came. Sometimes I reacted emotionally, but when they started to overwhelm me, I pushed them into the vault and locked them up.

I thought of several occasions when someone, knowing I'd been hurt, would ask, "How are you doing?"

"Oh, I'm fine, fine."

About 90 percent of the time I got away with it. I got away with it mainly because I believed it. "Oh, I'm fine," I could say and put on a convincing smile. After all, I had "dealt with the pain."

Most of the time I didn't know the old wounds still festered. How could I? I had locked the pain deep inside, so I didn't feel it.

The closest I had come to unlocking the vault revolved around the death of my father. He had, without realizing it, rejected me in thousands of ways all through my life. I had wanted his love and approval. He was an alcoholic, sometimes violent, and a man who didn't know how to show approval.

I cried at the funeral, and the pain hurt deeply. Dad was gone, and I'd never be able to get the approval and acceptance from him that I had sought all my life. So I cried, and that was all right. After all, crying was acceptable behavior over the death of a parent.

In the weeks that followed, I'd feel tears near the surface when I thought of him. Or something would happen that would cause me to remember a childhood incident that involved Dad—always sad events and always memories of rejection.

How did I respond? I stuffed more pain inside the vault. *Stop wallowing in your self-pity* was one of the things I told myself.

I thought I was being helpful. Now I realize the cruelty of those statements to my inner self.

But the pain didn't stay locked away. The long walk in darkness forced a level of self-awareness that I needed but didn't want. God had plunged me into deep darkness, and I saw no way out.

For the first time, I realized that darkness haunted my own soul. That was one of the hardest truths I've ever faced about myself. I had hidden away the hurts so efficiently that I had no conscious awareness of their existence. But the issues stayed with me.

Still unaware of those old wounds, each day I prayed for God to strip away the self-delusions. One of those delusions was that I handled rejection easily, that I didn't hurt and that I had worked through my troublesome issues.

As I slowly opened the heavy vault, my grief was horrendous. I realized that I had become an expert at self-delusion. Instead of opening the vault completely, I asked, "Why is God doing this to me? Isn't it enough that I've been living in spiritual blackness for months? What more does God want to do to me? How much more of this pain can I take?"

For probably an hour I gave God a terrible, angry tongue-lashing, and one of my recurring sentences was, "I trusted You, and You've let me down!"

I got no better.

Finally, I went to see my friend David Morgan. He talked compassionately with me and gently rebuked me for the unkind words I had said about my wallowing in self-pity. "This probably has more to do with your lifelong rejections," he said, "than it does with this situation."

As soon as I heard David's words, I knew what he meant. I felt like a child being rejected at school. I experienced again the pain when my dad turned away from me through my growing-up years. I thought of Lois, the girl I had fallen madly in love with when I was 15. She not only rejected me, but she also asked me to fix her up on a date with Chuck, my then-best friend. At various times, members of the church had coldly rejected me. The worst was a man who screamed, "You're the worst pastor I've ever known, and if anyone doesn't belong in a leadership role, it's you!"

The memories hurt. They flashed through my consciousness so rapidly that probably less than a minute passed. Without knowing it, I had opened the vault and seen what I had stored inside.

I didn't know how to cure the pain. Once the vault was opened I determined that no matter how much suffering I went through, I wouldn't slam it closed again. I didn't know how to handle the ongoing torment, but I couldn't give up.

Unable to sleep well that night, at about 3:00 A.M., I got up and went for my morning run. When I raced through a darkened neighborhood with malfunctioning streetlights, I felt as if my outward circumstances mirrored my inner turmoil.

Just then, and without warning, a single sentence flashed into my mind: *I have to feel them to heal them.*

I repeated that sentence several times before tears streaked down my cheeks. The inner hurt had come to the surface. When I reached the nearby park, I sat on a bench and let the tears flow freely. For perhaps 20 minutes, memories of rejection after rejection seeped through my brain.

Then a sense of peace came over me. The pain was gone.

I don't know many times when I've hurt more. But I knew that by experiencing that pain, God had been answering my prayer. He had stripped away one layer of self-delusion—the delusion that I could handle and had handled all my rejections.

—⁂—

"Lord Jesus, I don't know how many more
layers You have to strip away," I said, "but do it.
Keep on working in me."

13

PROTESTING INNOCENCE

One wintry afternoon, I was alone at home. My wife had gone to an overnight retreat. I had no social obligations, and I didn't want to see anyone anyway. For months I had been walking in the starless night without God turning the lights back on.

Okay, I remember telling myself, *I'm going to pray and open myself to God. I'm going to keep at it until I figure out what's coming between God and me, and then I'll get it straight.*

I prayed for a long time, for me—maybe a couple of hours. I confessed every sin I could think of. I went all the way back to childhood and tried to find any failures or acts of disobedience I could. I dealt with sins by category, such as jealousy and anger. During that miserable time, no answers came. I wasn't ready to give up. I confessed and re-confessed anything that I thought might unclog the obstruction between God and me. If it had been possible for me to force tears from my eyes, I would have done that.

Nothing came. Silence filled the room.

In desperation, I pulled out several Bibles. I like to use a variety of translations, so I flitted from one to another. I wanted to have words leap out at me and hear from God that way, but I didn't know where to read. I turned to my favorite New Testament passages, but they offered me no help.

Exasperated, I decided to let my Bible fall open anywhere and I would start reading. I'm not one for doing that kind of thing, but I wanted to read somewhere. I began with Psalm 17: "I am innocent, LORD! Won't you listen as I pray and beg for help? I am honest! Please hear my prayer" (v. 1, CEV).

"Innocent?" I couldn't believe what I had read. To check it out, I opened three other translations. They had translated the words a little more softly, but the intent was the same. A man who believed himself innocent and honest was crying out to God.

"I'm a faithful Christian. In every way I serve Jesus Christ. I'm right with everyone I know and there is no unconfessed sin in my life."

How do such statements strike you? A bit presumptuous at least; maybe even self-righteous; or probably the words of a self-deluded braggart. After all, who are we to boast of our goodness or faithfulness?

Or maybe part of the problem is cultural. We feel that we have to couch our statements of faith and commitment with a number of all-inclusive statements, such as the following: Despite being always a sinner and never fully aware of my own motives, I'm a faithful Christian, or at least I hope I am. In every way that I'm aware of—and I don't want to brag or bring dishonor to God—I serve Jesus Christ, even though I know I fail quite often.

As I've thought of those two approaches, I've wondered if there isn't some kind of middle ground. Is there a way for us to speak positively about our relationship with God without coming across as self-righteous to others and at the same time not sounding like some super-humble individual to ourselves?

My statements weren't quite so self-effacing, but I was so afraid that people might consider me boastful or hypocritical. And in our culture we dislike those people who have to tell us how sincere or spiritual they are.

Reading the Bible

During those months of my spiritual eclipse, I changed my mind about taking the self-effacing attitude. About halfway through the darkness (and of course I had no idea it was halfway), I began to read the Bible more fervently than ever. It wasn't a hunger that drove me, but a determination that if I ever was going to make it through the darkness, God would have to take me through. My prayers seemed to get me nowhere, and I felt that everything I said sounded as if I were trying to talk God into something.

On that wintry afternoon—and by then it seemed as dark outside as it did in my heart—I turned to the Bible with that determination to read it and keep on reading until I reached the light once again.

Why the Bible? For me, it remained the only connection I felt I still had with God. And I also sensed that it was the way God would finally speak to me.

Consequently, for the past few weeks I had spent more time reading the Bible than I had in years. Although I had no sense of the Holy Spirit active in my life and had been convinced that somehow my sins or my hardness of heart had alienated me, I had to do something to get back on track.

I read. Many times I saw words on a page, and when I finished a chapter I'd have to ask myself what I'd read. At other times, each sentence seemed to leap out at me—that was the rare experience. My reading especially centered on Psalms and Proverbs, and when I read Lamentations, I identified with the pain and discouragement of those five chapters. I have no idea why I selected those three books—none of them had been portions I'd particularly resonated with before.

I stayed for days at a time reading Lamentations again and again. Some days I'd focus in on the practical wisdom of Proverbs, but most of all I read the psalms. For quite a long time I wasn't aware of any internal changes. Yet something was going on—like the humming of background noise when the computer's making changes that we can't see.

Late that wintry afternoon, something did happen. It was a breakthrough for me. It came about as I read Psalm 17 several times.

Here, the writer, probably David, says quite forcefully that he's innocent. He makes no side statements to talk about his innate sinfulness or to apologize so people won't think he's boastful. He's writing from the anguished cry of a hurting heart.

In reading it I thought, *Yes, that's how I feel as well. In my heart I'm as right with God as I know how to be.* That was as close as I could come to making absolute statements about my righteousness.

Here are some of the poet's statements:

- "I am innocent, LORD!" (v. 1)
- "I am honest!" (v. 1)
- "Only you can say that I am innocent, because only your eyes can see the truth" (v. 2).
- "You know my heart . . . and found me innocent" (v. 3).
- "I have made up my mind never to tell a lie" (v. 3).
- "I don't do like others" (v. 4).
- "I obey your teachings and am not cruel" (v. 4).
- "I have followed you, without ever stumbling" (v. 5, *CEV*).

As I read and reread those statements, they boggled my mind. Of course, my first instinct was to say, "Well, of course, that was

David writing. He was a man after God's own heart, and the model of Old Testament piety."

And yet David was human like everyone else. *Like me.*

It helped me to ask, *But what if David didn't write those words? What if some unknown and never-recognized poet penned this prayer?* Even if David wrote them, what if those words were meant to convey universal truth, and God never intended the psalm to be read only as the cries of one man in a particular situation? What if that writer penned words to give voice to all hurting people who cry out to God in their pain? What if those words speak for the sincere souls who seek answers? *What if that voice is my voice?*

As usual, I had to wrestle with comparing his situation with mine. His was probably life-threatening, and the enemies of God were upon him. And my life, by comparison, seems problem free and easy. He spoke about his mortal enemies surrounding him (v. 9) and being tracked down.

But what would it mean, I asked myself, *if the writer refers to interior anguish? What if his pain is similar to my anguish? What if he put into writing the searching, internal issues that I struggle with right now?* If that's true, I had found someone who understood. I had read the words of a man who wrote a psalm that encapsulated cries of my own heart. Of course, that's how Christians have always interpreted the Bible. We call that applying the truths.

I knew that, and yet I had never applied such honesty, such a profusion of innocence before. True, when I read promises and assurances of God's love, when I dwelt on verses about forgiveness and service, I had no problem pulling them out of the pages of antiquity into my modern setting.

But this time it was different. He claimed *innocence.* He says, "God, I don't deserve this kind of treatment." This man has searched his heart and cries out to God. In effect he's saying, "Okay, Lord, examine me and show me if I'm wrong. But unless You know otherwise, I come to You as one who is faithful, who seeks You, and who is innocent."

No matter how we read Psalm 17, the words come across as sincere and ring with genuine piety from the depths of the man's soul.

That's the first part: Here I am—a person fully committed to you. Then he goes on to appeal to God to hear him. He says, "You know my heart, and even during the night you have tested me and found me innocent" (v. 3, *CEV*). From that I infer that David had already done much soul-searching through sleepless nights because the heaviness of his heart kept sleep away.

For me the message said, "Oh, God, I stayed awake during the hours of darkness, searching my heart, and You've made me know that my heart is right with You."

As I thought about those verses and read them again and again, I felt comforted—some of the first comfort I had sensed from God in a long time.

"Yes, yes." I sighed in relief and said, "That's it exactly." I had turned to God in the beginning because of the overwhelming spiritual darkness. No matter where I looked, I saw no guiding light. For months I had been on a relentless search, scrutinizing my failures and peeking into the dark corners. Obviously I had failed God. Surely I had done something wrong, or why else would the face of God be hidden from me?

Farther Down the Path

I'm quite aware that I have an amazing capacity for self-deception. So not being aware of sin didn't mean it wasn't there. It meant I had to dig deeper.

Psalm 17 changed that. By eight o'clock that wintry evening, I knew I had moved quite a distance down the path out of darkness. It wasn't my failing or my wrongdoing that had plunged me into darkness. No matter what was going on, it wasn't because of sin or deliberately choosing not to follow God.

The darkness didn't lift, but something did change for me. I could lift my head again. I stopped the constant scrutinizing. It brought me to a place where I could say to myself, *Whatever is going on, it's not my actions. This is in God's hands.*

Well into the evening hours, I leaned back in my chair and closed my eyes. I felt a calmness I hadn't experienced in a long time. I still had no idea why God's face wasn't shining on me. But I did know it wasn't because of my disobedience or sinful behavior.

I also realized something else—the psalmist's protestations of innocence didn't end the chapter. I felt as if the writer and I had arrived at the same point.

The psalm ended with words of comfort for me. "As for me, I will be vindicated and will see your face; when I awake, I will be satisfied with seeing your likeness" (17:15).

I'm not altogether certain what the writer meant. A few scholars have assumed that the words "when I awake" refer to resurrection. That may be so, but there's so little in the Old Testament about any concept of life after the grave that I doubt he intended that meaning.

I like to think that after a good sleep he would waken refreshed and filled with joy and a consciousness of the divine presence in his life. Scholars might not like my version of that verse, but it gave me peace. I envisioned David as preparing to sleep. He had searched his heart and concluded that he was right with God. He believed that when morning came, all the negativism and despair would be gone.

Maybe that was more a prayer from my heart than an explanation of the verse, but it gave me peace. I fell asleep in my chair. When I awakened after midnight, I didn't see God's face or feel any kind of mystical presence. But I knew I had crept forward, even if only a little. I hadn't figured it out yet, but I knew with certainty that whatever was going on, it wasn't because my sins had displeased God.

"Thank you," I whispered into the darkness as I lay my head on the pillow.

—◆—

I knew the darkness would go away eventually and
God's face would shine on me once again.

14

GOD'S SLEEP

Don't we admire those who can push aside all the stress, and sleep peacefully? But when we read in the Bible that God sleeps—or so it seems to us—that disturbs us. God is supposed to remain awake, stay vigilant and always remain alert on the job.

Divine vigilance makes me think of the giant eye we find on U. S. dollar bills. Regardless of its origin or original intent, that's a picture of God that I like—the all-seeing eye, the One who never misses anything going on in the world.

Sometimes I like to think of God as being like watchmen in the Old Testament. Those men, hired to stay awake all night, walked around the city walls, constantly observing, ever investigating any suspicious sound. If any danger came, they sprang into action and sounded the alarm. During the grape harvest, farmers hired guards to sit in a tower to prevent foxes or other animals from stealing the fruit. If they grew lax or fell asleep, great quantities of their fruit disappeared.

And yet, despite God's ever-watchful eye, several times in the Old Testament the writers cry out to God, "Wake up, God! Stir yourself!"

Not for a second do I believe they thought that God napped. For them it was a way of expressing how they felt. In their loneliness and fear it appeared *as if* God had fallen asleep. Bad things had happened to them, and there had been no warning and no deliverance in those dark moments.

If trouble piled on top of trouble and they saw no divine intervention, they used the image of God being asleep. They appealed to the Covenant Maker who had promised always to be with them, to bless their crops and to give them long life in the land. But when they surveyed their lives, there were certainly times when the promises didn't seem very significant.

I understood the plaintive wail when I read, "Awake, Lord! Why do you sleep? Rouse yourself! Do not reject us forever. Why do you hide your face and forget our misery and oppression? We are brought down to the dust; our bodies cling to the ground. Rise up and help us; redeem us because of your unfailing love" (Ps. 44:23-26).

"That's it! That's it exactly!" I said as I read the verses over again. The writer must have felt that God had turned away. It was a cry over God's inattention or aloofness, and he couldn't cope with that.

How well I identified with those words. I wanted God to get involved in my life in an obvious, tangible way. What I couldn't see—and could only accept by faith at the time—was that God was actively involved in my life. Even more, God was quietly directing my life. I couldn't see the action in the midst of darkness. (What can anyone see in total darkness?)

My faith, however, enabled me to say, "Wait a minute, none of this dark stuff caught God by surprise." That wasn't the problem in this psalm. The writer didn't cry out because God didn't know, but because God hadn't acted at the time or in the way in which he wanted God to act. God hadn't snatched the people out of their turmoil, or at least hadn't given them light for the pathway.

"Act, God! Do something." That's what they were saying. "Don't make us keep waiting."

Doing Enough

I understood. Those words express the pattern of most of my life, and I think that's the overarching message of Western Christianity. Why sit in silence when we can do something productive? Something helpful?

Much of Western thinking is built around productivity. If I do enough, it shows I'm good enough. Consequently, the busier we stay, especially in serving Jesus Christ, the better Christians we must be.

It doesn't work quite like that.

For several years I struggled over that very issue. I had slowly begun to accept that I was worthwhile in the sight of God simply because I was alive—a created being of God. I had slowly agreed on a visceral level that I didn't have to do anything except be myself.

Then darkness fell, interrupted that process and some of the old fears and images arose again. What did I have *to do* to get things turned right? Once I finally admitted there wasn't anything I could do, I turned more fully to God.

"If the Lord is aware of all this," I said in a moment of clarity, "and my faith says He is, then—thinking like those weeping poets of the psalms—I also have to say that God orchestrated the events. Not my sin, not the work of spiritual enemies, but my heavenly Father, for purposes I couldn't grasp, has brought this upon me. Even in darkness I am where I am by divine appointment."

By divine appointment? By God's plan and in fulfillment of His purpose? I nodded and said, "Yes, I believe that."

That led me to the next question. If God has thrown me into the den of lions, what's next? My reading the Old Testament helped me grasp that the people of God saw their hardships, suffering and pain as coming from God to make things right in their lives. He was like a loving-but-disciplining father who wanted to make things right once again. Sometimes they had to suffer a little before they could enjoy the blessings.

That made sense when I looked at the ancient records. It helped that even though they understood, it didn't erase their anxieties or destroy their fears. Like me, hundreds of years later, they found nothing but the absence of God's smile. "Why do you keep looking away? Don't forget our sufferings and all our troubles" (Ps. 44:24, *CEV*).

What makes the psalms so potent is that they illustrate what God had told them to do in their times of trouble—to cry out "Help, Lord!"

That's what I did—not from lack of faith or discouragement as much as from the realization that only God could help.

When I read the exhortation, "Awake, O Lord!" it said two important things to me. First, it was a cry of despair. "I'm at the bottom; I can't help myself. If You don't deliver me, I'm finished." Second, it was a cry from the innocent who must accept their circumstances.

A Cry of Despair

I remember a story told me during the years of the cold war by a man named Richard. He had been born in Russia, had grown up in Poland and escaped to the West. As a young man, he became a Christian and wanted to help his own people. He got tourist visas and went to Russia regularly and preached in underground churches.

One night he was on a plane flying from Moscow to Geneva. More than two-thirds of the passengers were part of a group of avowed atheists—men and women who worked to destroy evangelical Christianity in the then Soviet Union.

An hour out of Moscow, bad weather struck, and the plane rose and fell unexpectedly in the clouds. People screamed, certain they would crash. Richard sat in the last row of the plane. He was scared, but he sat there, strapped in his seat, and with his eyes closed, he silently prayed for peace.

More noise erupted with increased screaming and crying. Richard looked up and saw several of those Russian leaders kneeling in the aisles, crying for God to save them. They pleaded for mercy and forgiveness.

Eventually, the plane passed through the storm, and the officials once again resumed their stoic positions, and Richard said no one would have known or believed what he had witnessed only minutes before. But in desperation, even those who don't claim to believe reach out for help beyond their rational world.

That may be the kind of praying of the writer of Psalm 44, but I think it's much deeper. I think he cried out—not from desperation or from fear of dying—but he cried out *because of faith*.

He believed. He expected God to intervene, to deliver, to rescue them from danger. Why wouldn't God snatch them from evil or harm? It was more a prayer of awareness of God's silence or inactivity. It was a cry of "Where are You? When are You going to save us?" Only those who believe in a loving, caring, all-powerful God would pray that way. They expected God's help. It was the absence of help that discouraged them. The Russians, on the other hand, probably hadn't expected God to do anything, but it was like covering all the bases. There might be a merciful God.

It's the kind of prayer that comes from the hearts of those who have exhausted all their own resources and energies, and now they know they have only one other place to find help.

A Cry from the Innocent

A second thing occurred to me while reading this psalm. Although it contains a number of personal elements, it's essentially a psalm about national defeat. The verses help me realize that sometimes the innocent have to suffer for no apparent wrongdoing. Psalm 44, perhaps more than any other chapter in the book, contains the clearest example of a nation in search of a cause for national disaster other than guilt and punishment. The writer tells of divine victories and that it was the Lord who drove out the enemies.

As I continued to think about God's sleep, I followed the message of the psalmist where he goes on to add, "But now you have rejected and humbled us; you no longer go out with our armies. You made us retreat before the enemy" (44:9-10). The writer paints picture after picture of desolation, and God isn't on the scene. He justifies the people by saying, "All this came upon us, though we had not forgotten you; we had not been false to your covenant" (v. 17), and says that the people didn't turn away or stray.

Then I read what, for me, was the most potent statement—they recognized this as God's activity—the active, non-sleeping God: "But you crushed us . . . you covered us over with deep darkness" (v. 19). Yes, I understood that.

As I continued to think of that psalm, it made me realize a truth I didn't like to acknowledge: God might actually be teaching us through the lessons of defeat. Who wants to hear such a message? And yet, too often that's how we learn, isn't it?

It reminds me of once when I sat in on a meeting of Alcoholics Anonymous. One person spoke of several attempts to gain sobriety without success and added, "I failed a number of times and finally realized that I learned through my failures."

"That's the only way we learn," quipped someone else.

I disliked hearing that, maybe because it's closer to the truth about life than I'd like to admit. Maybe it says a great deal about me and countless others: defeat, falling on our faces and admitting we can't win on our own is what ultimately makes us victorious.

I prefer to believe that by remaining faithful, watchful and sensitive to the Spirit's guidance, I'll grow and continue on the path of maturity. That's what I want to believe. I don't think the person who said "the only way" was right—and we do learn by positive, forward steps. I'd hate to follow a God who did nothing but slap my wrists and say, "No, that's wrong."

I much prefer to think that God's Word is a light to my path and that I obediently go forward a step at a time. Unfortunately, reality sets in, and I have to accept that my loving Father uses both methods—those of success as well as failure.

As a teacher I know that encouragement and pointing out even the smallest achievement can enable many students to progress. When I taught sixth-grade below-average achievers, I worked with that principle in the forefront. Instead of trying to make them spell 25 words a week, we began with 10. Ten led to 12. By the end of the school year, with the exception of two pupils, the class had come up to grade level. They did it primarily because they succeeded first in small achievements. Small victories led to larger ones. Most of them had considered themselves dummies and failures. It took success—even in small measure—to move them toward believing they could achieve.

That kind of argument has always been my defense against getting knocked flat on my face. Besides, it's painful to fail. I hate it when God makes me or allows me to kiss the dirt. But those things happen to us—if we're willing to grow.

When We Fail

I'm convinced that we learn some lessons *only* by failing. Because the failure and the humiliation hurt deeply, we can't live with our shame anymore. We have to make changes.

I'll illustrate this with an embarrassing story about my childhood. I came from a family where anger was the most acceptable emotion for us. We screamed, yelled, raged and verbally spewed our venom over everyone near us. Then it was over and our anger collapsed. It worked in our strange, dysfunctional family and was the most normal behavioral pattern I knew.

After I became a believer I realized that was unacceptable behavior as an adult, but more especially as a Christian. I yelled at people several times; I lost my temper and said mean things; I erupted over seemingly small things. Each time I prayed for God's forgiveness. Each time I determined to control my anger and never let it happen again. But that didn't solve the dilemma. I became less volatile than I had been in my younger years, but still I spewed poisonous words that didn't please God.

Only later, after I faced the ongoing defeat in my life, did victory start to emerge. "God, I'm an angry man, and I come from an angry family. I'll keep messing up and hurting people unless You change me."

That's when the changes began—and they're still happening. Part of walking in the darkness for me was to see those failures in my life—those ongoing, agonizing defeats that kept me from full victory. Although I had been edging that way for a long time, during the silence of God, I faced that reality of helplessness.

Without God, I wouldn't change. Or to say it positively, only with God's help would I change.

Yes, sometimes God provides victory by taking us through defeat. Only when we realize that things aren't going to change, because we can't change ourselves, then God "awakens."

Light didn't burst through, the darkness didn't dissipate; but I had agonized in defeat and now called on the only power that could change me. When I did that—and with a fervency that comes only from repeated defeat—I sensed that I had moved a little closer toward seeing God's face shine upon me.

—⁓—

Although it may seem as if God is asleep when we
go through deep darkness, could it be that God is most
watchful in the moments of our despair?

15

"YOU OWE ME"

"God, You owe me!" I wonder how many of us have said such words. Not out loud perhaps, but I suspect we've harbored such thoughts. How many of us have sincerely believed that God has obligations to us? After all, we've left the sinful life and pledged ourselves to God's service.

I've felt that way at various moments in my life. I've prayed long and fervently, especially when I've wanted something badly. Then what I've prayed for doesn't turn out the way I wanted. Aside from a natural disappointment, often I have had stronger feelings. It's been, "I deserve this."

My attitude reminds me of a short-lived friendship with a boy named Gene during high school. He often invited me to have a Coke, occasionally to see a film, or sometimes we'd bowl together. Gene not only extended the invitation, but he insisted on paying. Obviously, he had more money than I did, and it made me uncomfortable. "I like doing it," he would say, "so let me."

After perhaps three months of our friendship, Gene's attitude began to change. He no longer asked, "Would you like to . . . ?" His invitation began, "Let's go . . ."

Although I heard the difference, I didn't think much of it or have any inkling where the relationship was going. Somewhere, the invitations changed to commands, "I'll meet you at 7:00 in front of . . ."

I didn't mind that either, because I liked the things he proposed. I accepted without question or objection—until one day in

April. I had a date with a girl named Carol, and it had taken me weeks to get up the courage to ask her out. She said yes, and we planned to attend a basketball game at school.

The day before my date with Carol, Gene and I walked down the hallway at school. "Tomorrow night we're going to the Orpheum Theatre," he said. "I've got us two good tickets to see the New York Touring Company's production of *Student Prince.*"

"I'd like to go with you," I said, "but I can't. I've got a date with Carol." He knew how long I had admired her.

"Yes, but this is coming to town only for two nights, and I've already got the tickets."

For what I remember as taking several minutes, I explained that I couldn't. Gene's anger erupted and he said, "Look at all the things I've done for you! Now you turn me down." In that instant, I saw what he had done. For months he had manipulated me, bought my friendship, and now he wanted to collect on his investment. Despite his saying all along, "I like doing this," his hidden agenda now came out, screaming, "I want to control you."

I had my date with Carol, and Gene never invited me to go anywhere with him again. A few days later, Gene had a new friend, and I never received more than a nod from him when we passed in the school hallways.

Relating that story reminds me a little of the way I found myself approaching God. I had surrendered my life to Jesus Christ in my early twenties and had followed Him ever since. When I wanted something—truly wanted something—I'm a little ashamed to say that I behaved much like Gene. I reminded God of my faithfulness in going to church, all the activities Shirley and I were involved in, my faithful giving; item by item I rolled out the Murphey Achievement List.

During the siege of the long night of God's hidden face, I faced what I had done. Once again it was reading one of those biblical passages that zapped me in the middle of my brain.

Of all places, the salvo struck me from Paul's letter to the Galatians, which seems like a strange source. I had grasped the theology of his letter years ago, but now I began to face the principle he espouses. Paul writes to Christians in Asia Minor after he learns that they have started to return to the Mosaic Law. They insisted that male converts had to undergo circumcision to be acceptable to Jesus Christ.

The thrust of the argument of the book of Galatians is that we are born into the family of God by faith and nothing else. If we try to add any other requirement, we nullify God's work of grace in us. Or put another way, if we add anything, we're trying to earn our salvation. If we earn it, then God must owe us something in return.

As I read the first four chapters of Galatians several times, I thought of the many times I had prayed for something I deeply wanted. If I had serious doubts about getting what I wanted, I often buttressed my request with a reminder of my faithfulness. Sometimes it would be as if I were saying, "Lord, I've been good for You, so now please be good to me." In my own way, I was behaving like Gene, or like the early Christians in Galatia.

It took me painfully serious heart searching to also change my attitude in my relationship with others. Too often, when I wanted a favor, I'd make the request and add, "Because . . ." That is, I'd give them a reason to grant what I asked. Maybe it spoke more about my insecurity and anxiety than anything else, but that was the way I did it. My *because* wasn't a blatant "You owe me," but it carried the same message. It was, I suppose, my way to justify my asking. That method often worked with people; it didn't seem to influence God.

At times, during my starless nights, I felt desolate. Asking God for something felt as if I had bought a lottery ticket and my chances of winning were about 1 in 50 million. If I had no assurance that God listened, how could I expect an answer?

A Different Approach

About the time I read Galatians, I also found a verse in the psalms that showed me a different way to approach God. "I wait for the LORD, my whole being waits, and in his word I put my hope" (Ps. 130:5).

At first, I thought about the waiting bit. That sure fit me because I had waited for months and no action resulted. After I read the end of the verse, I paused and reflected on it. Then, as if I had snapped on the electric lights, I saw the final phrase again: "and in his word I put my hope."

Hope in the Bible doesn't mean a wish or a vague desire, but a sense of expectation. That's exactly what I needed to read. *From now on, when I approach the throne of grace,* I thought, *I'll accept that it's useless to give God reasons to listen. I can't ever be good enough to earn the right to receive answers to prayer, but I can come with a sense of expectation. I can come because God loves to do good things for people. My sense of expectation also means I can approach because of God's faithfulness and because of the divine promises in the Bible.*

I thought of that hymn I had learned in the early days of my Christian experience, "Standing on the Promises That Cannot Fail." God's promises were self-commitments from heaven. I recall going for a long walk, and I spent most of that time repeating biblical promises of God. It would be God's faithfulness and God's unutterable word that would give me the courage and the expectation so that I could ask. Here are some promises I recited:

- "The righteous may have many troubles, but the LORD delivers them from them all" (Ps. 34:19).
- "Trust in the LORD and do good. . . . Take delight in the LORD and he will give you the desires of your heart" (Ps. 37:3-4).
- "No good thing does he withhold from those whose walk is blameless" (Ps. 84:11).
- "Ask and it will be given to you; seek and you will find; knock and the door will be opened to you" (Matt. 7:7).
- "Do not be anxious about anything, but in every situation, by prayer and petition, with thanksgiving, present your requests to God" (Phil. 4:6).

The list goes on, but I grasped the difference. The Lord doesn't owe me anything, but the promises enable me to discover the mind and purposes of God.

Paul penned these famous words in Romans as a divinely given promise: "And we know that in all things God works for the good of those who love him, who have been called according to his purpose. For those God foreknew he also predestined to be conformed to the image of his Son" (Rom. 8:28-29). In those two verses appear both promise and purpose. The promise is that everything that happens to us—everything—God uses for our good. The purpose is for us "to be conformed to the image of his Son" or, to say it another way, it's to make us like Jesus.

Hope pushed me to more fervent prayer. It wasn't easy or simple, but now I had a foundation—a solid one—on which to stand. Isaiah told the Jews of his day that their righteousness was like filthy rags, and I don't suppose mine was any better (see Isa. 1:18).

I also realized that my focus had been wrong. Too often I had looked inward with negative results when answers to my prayers didn't come. Or I had tried to manipulate God into giving me what I wanted.

This continued to be a struggle for me, even though I understood that I had something better than my achievement, faithfulness and commitment. I had the *immutable* promises of God. And if God promises, that makes it true.

I said this still proves difficult for me. My heavenly Father chooses to do good things for me (and for others as well), but at times I find it difficult to grasp that those acts of kindness have nothing to do with anything within me or anything I do.

In fact, it occurred to me that if I could find one reason for divine favor in my life, the Lord would owe me. I'm reminded of the words of Moses to Israel before they went into the Promised Land: "The LORD did not set his affection on you and choose you because you were more numerous than other peoples. . . . But it was because the LORD loved you" (Deut. 7:7-8).

The people of Israel never heard a reason for being chosen except that Yahweh loved them. We call that unconditional love, and that's difficult for many of us to accept—that we're loved in spite of all our good deeds and faithful doings.

True, we respond in gratitude and in service, but they're an effect and not the cause of God's caring. In my search for light I sensed I had already passed through the worst of the night's darkness. Nothing could be as bleak or as empty as what I had gone through. I had a growing assurance that my relationship with the Lord would be richer and more meaningful for me. Now I had God's word—God's promises that cannot fail.

Responsibility, Not Debt

God didn't owe me anything. I finally accepted that I hadn't earned or deserved any good thing that came from God. I took it one step further in my practical understanding. It came about because a friend had serious financial problems. He gave up a good pastoral position to work as a campus minister. Instead of a guaranteed income from a church, he had to depend on friends to contribute to his monthly support. The longer he remained a campus minister the lower his income dropped. He considered going back to a church, changing professions or doing part-time work on campus. My friend shared his dilemma with me and asked me to pray for him and his family.

One morning as I prayed, I thought, *God is responsible for him.* My friend hadn't called himself into campus ministry. He had stepped out only after he had sought guidance. He worked hard on a large campus and had begun to develop an ongoing ministry with Christian students who reached out to others.

I emailed my friend and said, "God is responsible for you. Maybe it's time for you to hold God accountable."

Even as I wrote those bold words to my friend, I realized they were words I needed to write to myself. (My friend held on, and within two months, he had enough ongoing support to continue his campus ministry.)

God is responsible for His own. That's not saying God owes us anything. Out of grateful hearts we've pledged ourselves to serve the Lord. When God accepts our service, it means a divine responsibility for us.

Then I thought, *I'm groveling in this dark dungeon because God thrust me here. It came about because I wanted to follow God more faithfully.* I also remembered the times when I'd sung the dedication hymns in church and pledged to follow Jesus Christ wherever He led me. My darkness wasn't the result of my sinfulness, but rather, God had pushed me into the dark place.

If God threw me into this den of night, I reasoned, *it's not my problem to get out.* I actually smiled when I thought, *I'm in the dark on divine assignment.*

"Wait a minute," I said aloud, "if this dark tunnel is God's will for me, why do I fret and stumble in confusion? God has to take care of me."

For most of my Christian experience, I had focused on my responsibility to do what God wants. I had cried out for help, for wisdom, for guidance—all the right things that Christians do. Now I felt I was in a different place. Now was the time for me to look seriously at God's obligations to me.

I wondered how the Israelites felt when they first encountered the Red Sea. The Egyptians were behind them, and a raging sea in front of them. Then the waters parted. Yahweh performed miracles to deliver His people.

The covenant-keeping God had called them out of the land of slavery; that same God was responsible to protect them and lead them into the land of promise.

I also thought of the end of the Israelites' journey into the new land. Those who left with Moses frequently cried out that their little ones wouldn't be taken care of, that they would perish in the desert. Instead, the little ones entered the land because God promised they would. Those who pulled back in fear and doubt died in their wanderings.

In the New Testament we read of Paul, the prisoner on a ship heading toward Rome. The ship is going to break into pieces and sink. The others panic, but Paul remains at peace. God told Paul that he would reach his destination and speak before kings. He could relax because he believed it was the divine will for him to reach Rome.

That meant God was responsible to get Paul to a place of safety and eventually enable him to reach the center of the Western world. Although the ship broke up and sank, no one on board drowned. God, who was responsible to fulfill the promises given, didn't fail.

"God is responsible for me." I no longer hinted that God owed me anything—and in my mind there is a serious difference. Because the Lord loves me, I will be cared for and provided for.

—₥—

God's provision is based on unconditional love—
not on my faithfulness. I was getting closer to the light.

16

FINDING GOD IN BABYLON

Once in a while, I'll read something in the Bible that shocks me—words or commands that make me pause and wonder how it could be.

For instance, the book of Habakkuk starts out with a big surprise. The Jews have failed God and sinned, and they will be punished. A more sinful nation, Babylon, will overpower them. "I am raising up the Babylonians, that ruthless and impetuous people" (Hab. 1:6); the rest of that chapter tells about the havoc that would result.

God uses evil people to punish His own people? No wonder the prophet says, "For I am going to do something in your days that you would not believe, even if you were told" (v. 5).

That had to be extremely difficult for the people to digest. But once the Babylonians had started to carry them into the land, Jeremiah gave them a message that sounded even stranger.

Here's the background: five centuries before the birth of Jesus Christ, the heathen raged at the gates of Jerusalem, and Jeremiah had to tell the Jews—God's special, holy people—that they wouldn't be delivered. What a blow that must have been for them! God had always pulled off a miracle, even if it was at the last moment. Habakkuk had already prophesied the message that they would have no deliverance, but they obviously hadn't believed it.

Back in the days of Hezekiah and the Assyrians, the city had almost fallen, but God intervened on two occasions to deliver the people, and the Assyrian armies fled in fear.

By the time of Jeremiah, a century later, the people hadn't repented, and God said no deliverance would come. The end is near. It must have been a difficult and painful message for the people to accept. In fact, most of the people refused to acknowledge that the Babylonians would defeat them, carry many of them into exile and completely destroy the great city of Jerusalem.

As bad as they had been in failing to keep the divine commands, a nation more evil than they were would pillage the city and carry them into a foreign land, so what were they to do? Where was the God who loved them? The God who spoke of loving them with an everlasting love? The God who promised they would be the chosen people forever?

If you or I were writing, we'd probably try to infuse them with courage. We'd remind them of the Lord's promises of faithfulness and point to the historical deliverance from Egypt and other victories over their enemies. We might even urge them to rebel and fight to the death.

Not Jeremiah. He thunders back an answer—but it's one of those unsatisfying responses: he tells them to find God in Babylon.

What a staggering statement that must have been for them to hear! Speaking for God, Jeremiah wrote: "Also, seek the peace and prosperity of the city to which I have carried you into exile. Pray to the LORD for it, because if it prospers, you too will prosper" (Jer. 29:7). He goes further by telling them not to listen to the prophets and dreamers who wanted to give them a different message.

Find God in Babylon? What a shock for them to read such words. They had been accustomed to visit the temple every week

and pray for the *shalom,* or peace, of Israel. They had always reacted with bitter cries to God for vengeance on those who threatened their lands or their people. Psalm 137 cries out against their
enemy, "Daughter Babylon, doomed to destruction, happy are
those who repay you according to what you have done to us.
Happy are those who seize your infants and dash them against
the rocks" (vv. 8-9).

And now the message of the prophet is to urge them to take a
giant leap forward and pray, not for vengeance, but for the well-
being of their enemies!

Some scholars have called this the beginning of a new spirituality. The words given show a struggle against a narrow, national-
istic view of the Jewish faith. Eventually that kind of spirituality
finds its ultimate message in the words of Jesus: "You have heard
that it was said, 'Love your neighbor and hate your enemy.' But I
tell you, love your enemies and pray for those who persecute you"
(Matt. 5:43-44).

But they weren't ready for that kind of message from the
prophet. What a painful, disheartening sermon for them to have
to hear. Now they're supposed to change their attitudes and *pray
for* the Babylonians instead of *work against* their captors.

I read Jeremiah 29 when I was desperately seeking a way out of
the darkness. In a sense, I felt as if I had been taken captive and exiled in a strange country. "What do I do next?" I had the same tor-
tured question.

As I continued to seek God's hidden face, Habakkuk's message became more obvious to me. My immediate goal was simple—
I had to find God in Babylon. Or to make the application clear, I
had to discover God in the place where I was right then—deep inside the darkness. I had to come to terms with my situation, but

more than come to terms, I felt God was mandating me to make the most of it. Maybe even enjoy it? No, I didn't think God wanted me to go that far.

But I didn't want to apply that message to myself. How could I find God when I was too miserable to do anything except hug my knees in pain as I wailed for deliverance?

I read Jeremiah 29 several times and couldn't get beyond that section. Later on, I was able to find the oft-quoted promise in verse 11, which we adapt too eagerly without reading the context. First, they were to find God in Babylon, and then they heard what would happen after their 70 years of exile were completed: " 'For I know the plans I have for you,' declares the LORD, 'plans to prosper you and not to harm you, plans to give you hope and a future. Then you will call on me and come and pray to me, and I will listen to you'" (Jer. 29:11-12).

I saw the situation clearly. If I wanted to inherit the promises, I had to follow the command. If I would find God in the dark place, I would see the promises fulfilled for my future.

In the first seven verses of chapter 29, the Lord makes it clear that they were in Babylon by divine decision: "This is what the LORD Almighty, the God of Israel, says to all those I carried into exile from Jerusalem to Babylon" (v. 4), and again: "Also, seek the peace and prosperity of the city to which I have carried you into exile" (v. 7).

Why did Jeremiah stress that God had taken them into exile (or captivity, according to some translations)? If he were living today, we'd want Jeremiah to soften it and say that God "allowed" them to be defeated and exiled; but the fiery prophet lays total responsibility on God. And, as I thought about it, wasn't that exactly the point the prophet wanted to make? The Jews needed to know that even in the terrible ordeals they had undergone, and the traumas that still lay ahead, God had brought it all about. And God had plans *beyond* the immediate defeat. They didn't end up in a foreign land by accident or because God blinked.

In a symbolic sense I understood this quite well. For months I lived in Babylon. I had been carried away from the things that brought me peace and comfort. I kept leaving messages for heaven, but God never returned my calls.

Then one day I pushed through the lengthy book of Jeremiah, trying to grasp the message (although I think my reading was more a way of saying to God, "I'm doing something. See? I'm seeking You through reading Your Word"). When I reached chapter 29, it was one of those times when I read the verses and knew God intended me to read them, understand them, accept them and apply them to my life for guidance.

I had to find God in Babylon.

"How do I do that?" I asked.

Immediately the obvious answer came back to me: the same way the ancient Jews did.

Prayer for Others

And what way was that? Simple. At least it was for those who listened to Jeremiah and obeyed God's voice. They prayed for those in power over them; they sought the welfare, or the good, of their captors. Not for a minute did I think God was saying, "Forget about yourself and concentrate on others, and all will work out for you. If you pray for your enemies and people around you, I'll bless you."

I did hear the mandate to pray for others. I began to do it more faithfully and systematically. I made what I call prayer contracts with people. When they expressed needs, I'd say, "Okay, I'm going to pray specifically for you for the next 30 days." I would also make it clear precisely what I would pray for.

As important as that was for me (and I don't mean to downplay it), I "heard" a stronger message. I had to find God—discover God afresh—in Babylon. As I surveyed my life, and it seemed as if God had vanished, I still had to keep looking.

This time, however, I sensed I would find God in a different way. As I meditated on my life, I wondered, *What if my circumstances don't change? What if I have to walk in the starless night from now on? What if the Holy One's face never shines on me again? What will I do?*

I would have to do what the exiles did—stay right there and forget about a trek homeward to Jerusalem. For them, Babylon had become home. They may have longed for Jerusalem, but most of them died in Babylon during the next 70 years.

Finally it became obvious: I had to accept my circumstances as they were. That may sound rather simple, but it wasn't. Until then I had thought of my walk in the dark night as a temporary experience. A few weeks, six months maybe, and then the warm, soft lights of dawn would streak across the horizon.

Like a lot of other Christians, I used to read and focus on the verse of promise. In Jeremiah 29:10, God gives the exiles assurance that things were temporary: "This is what the LORD says: 'When seventy years are completed for Babylon, I will come to you and fulfill my good promise to bring you back to this place [Jerusalem].' "

Seventy years seemed like a long time, but it was still a promise that said, "It won't always be like this."

This promise follows: "You will seek me and find me when you seek me with all your heart. I will be found by you and . . . will bring you back from captivity" (29:13-14).

Even though I read those promises, I couldn't move my concentration beyond the command in 29:7 to stay in Babylon and accept my life as it was. I had to face a reality that light might never shine again. If that sounds dark and pessimistic, I didn't feel that way. For me it was a message of hope. I couldn't change my environment, my circumstances or force God to act. The only thing I could do was to make some changes in Cec.

Those changes began with acceptance.

The apostle Paul said it in 1 Thessalonians 5:16-18: "Rejoice always, pray continually, give thanks in all circumstances; for this is God's will for you in Christ Jesus." I had quoted those verses many times, but now they became the words I needed to apply to my situation in Babylon. Rejoice? Pray? Give thanks? I had concentrated on "Get me out of here" and "Let's move on." I had hardly stopped to rejoice and give thanks. That was where I needed to start.

Even then it wasn't easy, because I didn't feel like rejoicing or praising God. I didn't have any desire to rejoice, and I didn't see much to praise God about.

What works for me may not work for others, but I decided to move in two directions. First, each day I would say that I accepted my life the way it was. I didn't have any emotional pleasure behind the words, but I did have a commitment to accept my life. "This is where You want me; I accept myself and my situations as they are."

Next, I wanted to be thankful and praise God for all the blessings of life. But when my emotional temperature registered 50 degrees below freezing, I felt spiritually frozen. "If I could give thanks, I probably wouldn't be here anyway," I said.

"Give thanks in all circumstances." That phrase kept coming to me. I don't believe it meant to give thanks *because* of being there, but it was a way of saying that no matter where I found myself, I could give thanks.

Giving Thanks

I started. Each morning before I got out of bed, I lay there and counted a minimum of 10 things for which I was genuinely thankful. The first few mornings it took quite an effort. I decided I wouldn't overlook even the tiniest things or experiences.

I was healthy. I had a wonderful wife. The relationship with my three kids was affectionate. I paused then and kept thinking. I was thankful that I do the kind of work I enjoy. Months earlier I had bought a new car, and I thanked God for that. Small things. Everyday things, but all of them fit under "in all circumstances." Several Bibles translate it, "in everything."

Even then I understood that when we're down, it's hard to appreciate the good. One thing I know about forming good habits is that you have to stay with them. I once read that if we want to form a habit, we need to stay at it every day for about three weeks. By then it becomes ingrained. I stayed with daily giving of thanks, even when I didn't feel thankful.

To my surprise, over the next few weeks, it got easier to tick off the blessings. Before long, I had upped my number. No big deal to lie in bed and say thanks to God for 10 or 20 things, people or events. But it was in the beginning. I had made an effort to see God in Babylon, even when there was nothing to see or touch. All my spiritual energy had gone into hibernation, but I wouldn't give up.

Yes, I found God in Babylon. That is, I went through the daily discipline of giving thanks and praying for others. Nothing happened outwardly. And I confess that I thought as soon as I started operating right, the smiles of heaven would glow. But nothing changed drastically. My spiritual pulse stayed low and my temperature hovered below freezing. Yet something did happen to me, something I can't express in any way except to say I gained a stronger sense of expectation.

I didn't know when or how, but I knew that *one day* God's face would shine on me once again. In the beginning, my praying and giving thanks had been mechanical, and I had done it in obedience. In time, the exercise took on an energy of itself. Giving thanks became a part of me.

Eventually, it spilled over into other times of my day. I'd hear myself giving thanks to God for trivial things such as a smile or kind word from someone at church, for unexpected moments of blessings. Yes, I had found God in Babylon.

Although I still walked in darkness, hope seeped into my system and diffused the despair. Maybe my "70 years" would end soon. Maybe God's thoughts of "plans to prosper you and not to harm you, plans to give you hope and a future" were for me after all.

As that thought struck me, I paused to give thanks to God for hope. I was still in Babylon. I might remain there the rest of my life. But I knew I wasn't alone or unloved.

—◊—

Even though God's face still remained hidden,
I knew He was working in my life.

17

NEEDED GUILT

I had done wrong—which I realized about two minutes after I had done it. The "what I did" isn't as important as what flowed after I acknowledged my failure. It had been a rather small thing. I had misunderstood something Ann, a Sunday School teacher, said to me. I took offense and lashed back at her with unkind, heated words.

That was only one way in which I had failed God and ended up eating guilt long into the night hours. That happened long after I had plunged into the deep pit of darkness.

Like many people, I often realize my sins and failures only later when I'm forced to rethink what I've done. That usually happens to me about 2:30 in the morning. I get to sleep (that particular night I didn't), then awaken to focus on things I haven't resolved. When that happens, it's as if my resistance has shut down and I'm vulnerable. My conscience troubles me, and guilt plays a shameful tune inside my brain.

I had already apologized to the woman I had offended, and she had forgiven me. Then why did I still feel guilty? As other songs of failure marched through my consciousness and I confessed to God immediately, it didn't seem to make any difference. The heaviness inside didn't go away or even diminish. I would become aware of something I had done wrong, confess it and minutes later I would go back and listen to the same stanza of the same mournful melody.

I was experienced enough in the Christian faith to realize an important truth: God had already forgiven me in Christ Jesus. The problem was mine; obviously I hadn't forgiven myself. I knew I needed to concentrate on being more self-loving and self-forgiving.

I didn't want to excuse myself, but I knew I had to push away the guilt so that I could allow compassion to flow toward myself. That didn't take place. The burden, if anything, became heavier. "By now, you ought to know better," my guilt-laden voice whispered. "You're no better at keeping your mouth shut now than you were 20 years ago."

Disgusted with myself and unable to sleep, at 4:30 A.M., I went out for my early-morning run. It was one of those badly overcast mornings so that no stars shone. "It's the way my life is going now anyway," I muttered as I started out. As my feet pounded the cement, my mind toyed with forgiving myself. "Oh, God, help me to be compassionate toward me," I pleaded again and again. "I feel so guilty. Take it away."

I had started my fourth mile when a powerful thought zapped me, and I said out loud, "Wait a minute. I need that guilt!"

The Challenge

For the next two miles, I realized the truth of that statement. What would have happened if God had merely dissolved my feelings of guilt? What if I had been able to say to Ann, "Hey, sorry," and then forgotten about it? Or if I had been able to say, "I forgive you, Cec"? I know exactly what would have happened. I would have committed the same sin again and not been very concerned about the consequences. I wouldn't have learned very much. In fact, I might have "learned" a wrong message about cheap and easy forgiveness.

In the middle of my dark period, I slowly came to terms with the value of my sense of guilt. At times it felt like a heavy lump inside my stomach that wouldn't dissolve. When I stayed busy, I didn't think about it. But as soon as I would get quiet or become reflective, guilt gnawed at me. It was simply *there*, and it demanded attention.

It wasn't going to go away.

I'd had that feeling before, of course, and had somehow worked through it. Most of the time in the past I'd agonized over the particular incident and eventually the passage of time softened the lump.

Now I had to think of guilt differently. If I needed to feel guilty, then how would it benefit me? What if this was the way God wanted it to work? I've always been one to get rid of guilt as quickly as possible.

Somewhere I picked up the idea that if guilt pursues us, it's not God at work but evil forces or our own harsh, unrelenting self that won't let go or give us grace. What if the guilt has a positive purpose? What if God wants that heavy lump to stay there for therapeutic reasons? What if I truly *needed* guilt?

That morning when I said, "I need the guilt," I thought for a long time about my past failures, especially the ones that had troubled me the most. A number of them struck me—the kind that stayed with me for weeks, sometimes months—before I could sincerely put them away or forget them.

Guilt Hurts

Those were hard times. I hurt. Usually I hurt alone, because I couldn't share the pain with anyone. I was too ashamed or embarrassed, or I didn't think my friends would understand, such as when my words wounded someone badly or when I became aware of insensitivity to another's needs.

My zeal was to get away from my failures and painful memories. That made me think of my friend Phil. For almost a decade he had lived on tranquilizers. As soon as the emotional memories of a dysfunctional childhood and alcoholic background pushed at him, instead of exploring them or trying to cope, he popped a pill to make the memories go away. And it worked.

That is, it worked as long as he continued to take the pills. Four years ago, Phil realized that medicating himself didn't cure anything—it gave him only temporary relief. He decided to ease himself off the pills.

It took him nearly six months, but he feels—he actually *feels*—his emotions. Some days he hurts badly, but as he said, "Now I can experience what I feel, and it's new to me. When I was on tranquilizers, I didn't feel guilt or anything. I lived in numbness. I'd rather feel."

Phil also reminded me of the days when I was a pastor. I also volunteered to do chaplaincy work at a local hospital. Whenever anyone died in the emergency room, the hospital had a rule that the attending physician or a head nurse, as well as a member of the clergy, had to be present to inform the family, which the nurses gathered into a small room.

In almost every instance, as soon as the doctor or nurse said, "I'm sorry, but Mr. Johnson expired"—they never said *died*—the crying began. Within seconds some family member would ask the doctor to give the surviving spouse a shot. In those cases the person who made the announcement didn't automatically pass out a pill or give an injection just because someone panicked.

One time in particular, an emergency ambulance had answered a 911 call about an elderly man with chest pains. He died on the way to the hospital. When the nurse said, "The doctor was unable to revive him," the adult children wailed with their grief. The widow dropped her head and cried softly. The children begged the nurse to medicate their mother. One daughter took two Valium from her purse.

"Can you handle this?" the nurse asked as she reached out and took the mother's hand.

The woman nodded.

"I can give you something if—"

"I don't want anything," the woman said. "After 53 years of being together, I want to sit here a few minutes and face my loss."

That took a lot of courage for the woman to speak up when her children wanted to medicate her. I'm convinced she did the right thing.

Thinking of Phil's decision and the widow's was essentially where I had arrived. Like them, I didn't want to ignore, deny or run away. In my case, I needed the pain to keep me focused on the problem.

Whether our problems are huge or minor, none of us likes the discomfort that accompanies them. Who wouldn't want to feel better?

I also realize that, like anyone else, I do things out of my sense of need, often an unconscious one. I may clamor for attention, but attention isn't the real issue. The problem—the need—may be that I don't feel loved or accepted.

Too often we tranquilize ourselves or distract our pain, but we cure nothing. The heavy lump in the stomach remains.

Although a part of me wanted to escape, to find a way to push away the discomfort, a stronger part of me whispered, "Let pain be a friend. Let it help you so you can learn more about yourself, so that eventually you will discover healthy ways to have your needs met."

I allowed myself to hurt.

Whenever I was tempted to feel sorry for myself or do something to lessen the inner discomfort, I would say aloud, "I face my pain. I feel my pain." That approach may not work for everyone, but it did for me. Slowly, the nagging guilt subsided.

Another Valued Lesson

One other understanding came out of this struggle with guilt. My thoughts went back to seeking God's hidden face. I realized something remarkably simple: I wouldn't have valued this lesson if God had smiled at me and said, "Go and sin no more."

The revelation of the need for guilt had come while I ran during the predawn hours. As I continued to run in the darkness that morning—literally and spiritually—that insight flashed through me. In the darkness, in the aloneness of the early morning, I didn't see God's face. I had no sense God was even around, but the thought, the insight—*what if that was my heavenly Father speaking to me through the overcast sky? Whispering to me through the darkness before dawn? What if the Lord was smiling at me through the clouds, and I didn't even know it?*

That morning it had been difficult to start my run. I thought, *Today is going to be like every other day.* Depression tried to grab hold of me, but I knew I always felt better after exercise, so I went out anyway. As I ran the first block, I heard myself cry the words of Cain, "My punishment is more than I can bear" (Gen. 4:13).

Before I finished my run I heard myself say, "I've gotten to know the darkness. I'm no longer terrified of the aloneness, of not seeing God's face. I know God's face is there, even though it's hidden from my sight."

Later that same day, as I continued to focus on my need for guilt, I recalled something said to me by my late friend Mike Tafel. "When life isn't going well, we beat up on ourselves a lot."

I understood because it has often been my modus operandi in trying to solve many dilemmas in life. If I'm not happy, it means I've sinned or done something stupid or didn't hear God correctly. I've also learned that my trouble comes not in the inward look but in the unkindness with which I search my heart. Guilt and failure overwhelm me, and I'm the handiest person to blame. This has brought about three important insights for me.

First, we're not kind to ourselves. We point a finger at ourselves, question our motives and see everything we do through the darkest pair of sunglasses.

Here's an example that is still fresh in my memory. One night, two of my writer friends and I went to an autographing at a bookstore. The novelist, who is one of my favorite writers, stayed afterward to chat with any of us who wanted to talk. Six of us hung around.

The man had published 10 books, and I had read seven of them and purchased my eighth. As we talked, I told him how much I liked his writing, and then I mentioned the last book of his I had read. "I liked it except for the ending. I thought you should have quit earlier."

He smiled graciously, shrugged and shifted into something else about his writing. As soon as the words had come out of my mouth, I heard how harsh they must have sounded. Besides, he hadn't asked for my opinion and obviously didn't want it. It didn't seem appropriate to apologize, so I kept silent.

But for the next two days guilt plagued me. I put myself under the bright light in the interrogation room. "Why did I say that?"

"I was being open and honest."

"Really? But what did you mean by that remark?"

I had to think about an answer.

"Was it disguised jealousy? Was it to show him your superiority as an astute reader?"

On and on the questions came until I sickened of the relentless interrogation. I finally said, "I forgive myself for saying such an unkind thing."

Second, we're too close to the scene of the crime. We don't have a lot of objectivity to stack next to our observations. Our past crime record has been indelibly imprinted on our brain. We haul out old records and say to ourselves, *Yes, and do you remember when you . . . ?*

It's like saying to myself, *Have another helping of guilt.* And I never refuse the offer.

Third, we lay more guilt on ourselves than we'd ask anyone else to bear. That's true. I'm harder on Cec Murphey than I am on anyone else. When a friend does something I don't like or understand, I may puzzle over it, rehearse it inside my head, but eventually I find a satisfactory explanation for the action. "He was tired." "She wasn't angry at me." "I happened to be there when he needed to let off steam." "She spoke up without thinking clearly."

I go into all of this because when I raced through the starless darkness in search of God's hidden face, my accusatory feelings peaked. Once again I had done self-critical analysis. Of course, I couldn't win. If I tried to explain myself or mitigate my actions, a nasty voice whispered, "You're trying to justify yourself." If I pleaded guilty, the same voice said, "See, that's the way you always are. You don't change or get any better, do you?"

There was no way for me to win.

Checking Motives

Even as I write this, it may sound as if I'm suggesting we avoid any self-viewing. Far from it. If my journey out of darkness has taught me anything, it's that although I experience the guilt—and acknowledge what I've done—I also need to look carefully at my motives. I need to look deep within and discover exactly what's going on inside me. I need to uncover my jealousies, anger and rejections.

But I can't stop there. Before I stop I have to wrap myself in self-compassion, to offer myself a little lovingkindness—as I would to a friend.

The only way I know to go through those steps of awareness to acknowledged guilt to extending compassion to myself is to have what we call a reality check. I do it in three primary ways.

First, I pray. But for much of that period prayer didn't seem to take me any place except further into a pit of isolation and guilt. The more I prayed, the more critically I looked inward and unkindly judged myself.

Second, I listen for God's voice to speak to me through the Bible. Even there I have to tread carefully. When I'm down in the dark valley, I tend to hear all the negative biblical verses aimed at me. For example, I read Jeremiah 17:9-10. It's hard enough to grapple with in most English translations, such as in the *New International Version*: "The heart is deceitful above all things and beyond cure. Who can understand it? I the LORD search the heart and examine the mind, to reward a man according to his conduct, according to what his deeds deserve." In the middle of my dark night I read those same two verses from the *Contemporary English Version*: "You people of Judah are so deceitful that you even fool yourselves, and you can't change. But I know your deeds and your thoughts, and I will make sure you get what you deserve."

I did, however, find that was the less common experience. Any number of verses brought comfort to me. A few days later, thinking back to Jeremiah's words, I said, "Okay, God, maybe I'm deceiving myself," and I read on.

The third form of reality check for me was to talk to the two people in my life who understand me. First is my wife, Shirley. I find it helpful to talk to her because she's a patient listener. Often she doesn't say a lot in response, but when she does, her cogent words get right to the heart of the matter for me.

The other person is my friend David Morgan. In his loving way he pushes me to get out of the menacing pattern of attributing the worst slant on my activities. He does a lot of what he calls reframing for me. He'll take the situation and turn it around so that I can view it differently. He reminds me that he loves and accepts me, and sometimes asks why I can't extend the same understanding toward myself.

I Needed That

Although I'm a couple of years beyond the darkness of night, I reflect and say without hesitation: *I need the experience. I need to feel guilty. I need to see myself in negative light as well as positive.* As much as it hurt—and it did—and as often as I went too far—and I did—it was part of the road I had to travel. Said another way, I needed a thorough examination of my motives and attitude. The big hurdle was for me to do that without plunging myself into despair or drowning myself in guilt.

About that time, I mentioned to an acquaintance at church that I was going through a difficult time, but I didn't elaborate. "Congratulations! It shows that God's at work in you," he said and walked on.

I stood there stunned. *Didn't he hear what I said? How could he be so heartless?*

Almost immediately, however, I realized that he had heard, and he wasn't going to dig me out of my pit. It was something I had to do myself.

As I continued to reflect on his words, I thought of Thoreau's statement: "The unexamined life is not worth living." My mind whirled with verses from the New Testament that said God was at work in me to will and do God's good pleasure (see Phil. 2:13).

That same week, I burned my arm on a hot skillet. It left a burn about half an inch long. I put something on it and it began to mend. Four days later it still hurt, a gnawing reminder of the burn, but I knew that was also part of the healing process. Then I thought, *sometimes it takes pain in our lives to bring about the healing.*

Despite my realizations and reality checks, the inner turmoil didn't go away immediately. I still struggled, but my friend David had helped me to reframe it—it was a form of spiritual therapy taking place.

—◊—

I knew I would get better.
I would accept and grow through spiritual therapy.

18

WHEN GOD STARES

"I can think of something worse," Ben Campbell Johnson said.

"I don't think so," I said. "The lack of God's response is about as hard as it gets."

Ben was then a professor at Columbia Theological Seminary. After he finished a series on spiritual growth at our church, he and I had coffee together. When he asked how my life was going, I told him about living with God's silence. "And I'm miserable with the silence."

"I know something worse than silence," he said. Without another word Ben leaned over, opened my Bible and pointed to Psalm 39:13. "Read it."

"Remove Your gaze from me, that I may regain strength, before I go away and am no more" (*NKJV*).

"That's worse," Ben said. "God's stare is a lot worse."

It took a few seconds for that to sink in. What's wrong with God's stare? Then I got it. It's a *scrutinizing* gaze, and who can stand up under it? Another translation puts it, "Look away from me, that I may enjoy life again before I depart and am no more."

"Yep, you're right."

When I got home, I thought more about what terrible agony David must have been going through when he penned that statement. It was as if God stared into the depths of his soul, and he couldn't take any more. Perhaps it was conviction for sin. I like to think that the divine scrutiny brought great discomfort because it forced David to see things about himself that he didn't want to see or know.

I understood that verse because I had experienced the stare through God's silence. Such moments can't be explained logically. They're those times when we're confronted by God in such a way that we can't make excuses, and we have no place to turn. His penetrating focus won't turn away, so we can only stare at the unrelenting gaze. The conversation with Ben changed my way of thinking. Instead of living under the eclipse, I thought of some kind of powerful, non-blinking eyes staring at me.

To feel God's perpetual stare feels worse than being convicted for sinful behavior. At least with conviction comes an awareness of having done wrong. The penetrating stare of God goes beyond actions or forms of behavior and settles on our being. And there's no escape.

As I meditated on that psalm, I thought of two New Testament incidents that illustrate what the passage said to me. One occurs in Matthew 8:28-34. Jesus travels in the area of the people called Gadarenes, and he delivers two demon-possessed men—two strong, violent men who had prevented anyone from passing that way.

Shouldn't that miracle have delighted the people? The fear is gone and they can travel where they wish. Yet the story ends with a note that all the townspeople, after hearing of the miracle, rush out to meet Jesus. "And when they saw [Jesus], they pleaded with him to leave their region" (Matt. 8:34).

It doesn't seem to matter that two men have been restored to their right mind. Instead of rejoicing, I suspect they fear Jesus—

not because He has done wrong but because He has done the powerful. He has brought light into dark places, and they can't stand that. Or as it says in John's Gospel about Jesus, "Light has come into the world, but people loved darkness instead of light because their deeds were evil. All those who do evil hate the light, and will not come into the light for fear that their deeds will be exposed" (John 3:19-20).

Perhaps that's why the gaze of God is so difficult for us to live with—it exposes to our own eyes what we don't want to see. That scrutinizing stare seeks out every crevice of our mind, and we don't like anyone—not even God—examining us that closely.

Luke's Gospel records the other story. At the Lake of Gennesaret, Jesus gets into Simon Peter's boat and tells him to go into the deep waters and let down his nets. Peter complains that they have been fishing all night but have caught nothing.

It's strange that Jesus, who had grown up as a carpenter, tells Peter, a lifelong fisherman, where to catch fish. Wouldn't most people resent such a demand? And it wasn't a suggestion either.

The response intrigued me. Peter says two significant things. First, "But because you say so" (Luke 5:5), and he lets down the nets. The catch of fish is so heavy the nets threaten to break.

Peter's second response comes after he sees the abundance of fish. He says, "Go away from me, Lord; I am a sinful man!" (v. 8).

Something powerful happens to Peter in that story. Luke records that Peter and his companions are "astonished"; but whatever happens to Peter exceeds astonishment. It's what I call a moment of enlightenment. There's a word, "epiphany," that says this well. It means a sudden, unexpected moment of enlightenment or understanding. That explains Peter's moment. A simple story, but a powerful effect enables Peter to see beyond the miracle. He realizes that the One who performed the miracle is able to stare into his soul.

In both of the New Testament stories there is a moment of instant awareness as if the brightest lights of heaven blot out all darkness. But the effects on the enlightened one are amazing. Instead of bringing joy, peace or contentment those moments can also frighten.

A Bad Reflection

Perhaps another way to say it is that when we look into God's face, we see ourselves reflected back—and that means we see our ugliness and our less-than-perfect lifestyle. I wonder if it's not a little like the shame that Adam and Eve felt in the garden. They had been naked all along. But after they had sinned and their Creator came to them, they saw themselves clearly. Their bodies hadn't changed—but they had been enlightened. They had an epiphany.

I've faced the staring God many times, and I've never found it pleasant or easy. I hated having the divine searchlight focused on me.

My thinking about Psalm 39:13 made me remember the cold stare that came from the penetrating blue eyes of Miss Irma Linder, my fifth-grade teacher. When her x-ray-endowed eyes and radar-enhanced ears fixed on me, I was done for. I couldn't lie, talk back or do anything except gulp and mumble, "Yes, ma'am."

Even today I vividly recall the fear that swept through my body when she peered at me over her heavy glasses. I dropped my head or looked away—anything to get beyond that cold, unswerving stare.

Even when I didn't know what heinous crime I had committed or that Miss Linder had found out about, I dropped my head, certain that she already knew everything. She never disappointed me.

It usually involved something I thought I had gotten away with—such as grabbing a quick drink at the water fountain when the class marched to the assembly room. Or chewing a piece of candy when she wasn't looking.

Once, she stood at the chalkboard writing, her back to the class. I whispered to Carol Miller across the aisle. I had already finished before Miss Linder whirled around, pointed her long, bony finger at me, called me by name and said, "Stay after school."

My memory of Miss Linder isn't too different from the concept of God I grew up with. I had tried Sunday School for a few months as a kid. But my teacher in that small church used no printed material, and we heard only a handful of Bible stories. After four or five Sundays, she repeated the stories. I was a bright kid with a good memory, so it didn't take long before I knew the stories and could finish telling them before she got past her introduction.

That wasn't the biggest problem. The issue for me was that she told the stories in such a way that I felt like an evil, sinful kid. No matter how good I had tried to be during the week, the Sunday School teacher had a way of evoking guilt and making me aware of how rotten I was. Although I heard about forgiveness, I didn't hear much about a loving, compassionate Savior. Whenever I walked into a church, I felt as if Jesus Christ secretly pointed a finger at me.

As an adult convert, I had to work through a lot of negative Christianity and move beyond the God who peers at everything I do, spies on me and waits to pounce on every infraction of the law.

Yes, I knew a great deal about the God who stares at sinners, but for a long time the One who loves sinners remained a stranger to me. Many times before my conversion I thought about my behavior, especially after I left home. Like any young man without a strong spiritual guide, I tasted widely of the enticing nectar of the world around me. But, even though I thought I had absorbed little of the church's teachings, whenever I did certain things, a terrible guilt overwhelmed me. I recall once wishing that God would mind His own business and not peer into my life all the time.

An Uncontrolled Tongue

After I became a Christian, I lost the overwhelming sense of the staring God. Well, once in a while it returned. It didn't happen when I fell into deep sin, because I didn't do anything that anyone would place in that category. Most of my moments of feeling the penetrating stare seemed connected to sins of the tongue.

Here's one instance. Shirley and I were sitting with our Sunday School class at the back of the auditorium for the final assembly. Across from me, three teenaged girls began to giggle in muffled tones. Before long they upped the noise level, and it turned into loud whispering and finally to loud laughing. I sat on the aisle, so I walked over to the major offender. I felt I spoke tactfully when I said, "Stop that! I can't hear what's going on, and you're disturbing me."

She shut up, and so did the others.

After the final prayer, Shirley said, "I wish you could have heard the tone of your voice when you spoke to that girl. It sounded mean."

"Mean?" I repeated in amazement. I hadn't felt mean, but my wife is a perceptive person who doesn't criticize easily. All the way home from church I said nothing. I kept thinking of my words to that girl. It took me 10 minutes before I could admit that *maybe* I had sounded mean. By the time we got home, after another 10 minutes of driving, I admitted to myself that Shirley had been right.

Why did that experience trouble me? Why didn't I simply dismiss it? I could have said, "Those girls needed a strong dressing down."

I couldn't get away from Shirley's remarks. Was that God staring at me? I'm not sure I had a sense of that then, but it was the same kind of thing. I had failed by hurting another person with my words—not with the message as much as the tone. (I called the girl and apologized.)

I think of another, more recent incident. I received a phone call from another writer. In the course of the conversation my words turned frosty. (Okay, they were freezing!) And she said, quite soothingly, "I think you're overreacting."

"Maybe you're right," I admitted, apologized and hung up a few minutes later.

As I sat beside the phone, I felt the stare of God, like Miss Linder's of old. If a heavenly voice had thundered, "You are the man!" I would have felt a little better. I didn't hear words of harsh judgment, but I sensed only the cold, silent stare. It was enough. I had gotten the call at ten o'clock at night and was already in bed. I couldn't sleep. I had apologized to the other writer, so that wasn't the issue.

The stare of God wouldn't leave. It reminded me of the TV traffic reports where the helicopter pilot says, "And this is your eye in the sky." I felt that eye in the sky's gaze focused right on me, and it wouldn't turn away. I tossed around in bed for a while before I dressed and walked in the dark for a couple of miles. Finally, peace came to me.

Perhaps such things too easily prick my conscience. I'm sure the legalistic threats of divine punishment in childhood have something to do with the staring-God concept. Maybe God isn't staring at me as much as I'm allowing a childhood threat to color my thinking.

Does the explanation make much difference? I think not. Maybe it's better that my loving Father has some kind of way to bring conviction to me. If it takes a silent stare to make me face up to my failure, I'm ready to come before God. I still want to drop my head, however, and I don't like the discomforting feeling.

As I envision myself before the Lord, my head lowered, it reminds me of stories in the Old Testament when people would come before the king with their heads bowed; they wouldn't dare look into his eyes. But if they found favor with the king, he would come to them. With his own hands he would lift their heads so they could see him.

I wanted to live with that image. Especially during those dark nights of my spiritual journey, I wanted to pray to the staring God, but I knew I couldn't face the penetrating gaze when I've broken divine laws in even the smallest way. So I'd cry out, "Lord, have mercy on me, a sinner."

Some nights I went to sleep aware of my inadequacies and failures. But as I got closer to the end of my dark period, that changed. One night, perhaps a month before the darkness began to leave, I felt extremely vulnerable. I felt too unworthy to look up at God.

A Loving Gaze

That's when I had a mental image—an epiphany perhaps. I could envision the hands of Jesus Christ touching both sides of my face. "Don't be afraid," I could hear Him say to me. This time the stare was one of love and acceptance. This time the gaze of my Lord was more like the way I look on my children or those I care deeply about. It's the kind of love that's obvious and real; it shows through the focused eyes.

That night I read my Bible and marked a verse that touched me: "You are the shield that protects your people, and I am your chosen one. Won't you smile on me?" (Ps. 84:9, *CEV*).

—ɯ—

The darkness was still around me, but for the first time
in all those long months, I sensed not only that God was out there
behind dark clouds but also that He was smiling at me.

19

UNHEALED PLACES

"Heal the parts of me that don't want to be healed."

What a strange kind of prayer.

Yet it was a prayer I heard coming from my lips. And as I listened to my own words, I knew I meant them. (I have no desire to share the specific nature of the problem, but I do think the principle is important when God turns off the lights and forces us into dark places.) It begins with awareness—perhaps an awareness that's always been there, but it's different this time. It's an awareness that makes us know we need to change—even when we don't want to change.

The best illustration I can offer outside the Bible involves my late brother, Mel. He was an alcoholic who died at age 48. He drank until a few days before he died. We lived nearly a thousand miles apart, but Mel often called during the last year of his life. Our conversations usually centered on God—something he had never wanted to talk about before—and each time he initiated the topic.

Even with serious mental deterioration, Mel had enough sense to know he needed help and that this help could only come from above. Many times he said he wanted to meet Mom in heaven and knew he would.

Despite those obvious desires for God, Mel couldn't let go of his alcohol. Or it may be more accurate to say, the alcohol never let go of Mel. Over the years he had tried to quit any number of times. He begged God to take the desire from him, but he always went back.

My brother was addicted. Just as our father had been an alcoholic, Mel had become one before he turned 20. I don't know why God didn't deliver him, but it may have had something to do with the double message of his heart. Yes, he wanted deliverance, but at the same time, he didn't. His addiction had such a powerful grip on him, Mel couldn't will himself to give it up. On the occasions when he stopped drinking, I think he knew it was always temporary. Mel wanted healing, but he never quite reached the place of asking God to heal the parts of him that didn't want to be healed.

Little Sins

To give a biblical example, I think of Saul, Israel's first king. He started out a godly man. He disobeyed the Lord in what seems to us like small matters, but they were enough that God said clearly that He rejected him and would raise up another king.

It's hard for us not to ask, "Why didn't Saul pray for God to change him?" My answer is that maybe he didn't have the will to fight the oppressing demons within.

I suspect that most (if not all) of us have those sins within that we don't want deliverance from, especially the little sins that we enjoy so much. Even godly, devout Christians get caught between two intense desires. What is it like to have two overwhelming passions, and they contradict each other? To feel God pulling one way but a different source pulling in another direction leaves us weary and defeated.

But it happens. In fact, it happens more than we care to admit.

As I pondered this concept, it began to sound like Joshua's final speech before his death. He calls the people of Israel together. He knows how easily they have gone astray in the past, so he reviews the history of the nation. Then he says, "Now fear the LORD and serve him with all faithfulness. Throw away the gods your ancestors worshiped beyond the Euphrates River and in Egypt, and serve the LORD. But if serving the LORD seems undesirable to you, then choose for yourselves this day whom you will serve. . . . But as for me and my household, we will serve the LORD" (Josh. 24:14-15).

The people give the right response: "Far be it from us to forsake the LORD to serve other gods!" (v. 16). They then talk of God's power at work in them.

If God is at work in those people all those years, how did they end up having to make a choice? They are the children and grandchildren of the freed slaves of Egypt. Most of them didn't see the workings of God themselves during the 40 years of wilderness wanderings. Some had been children when they started, others were born on the trek and others weren't born until after they entered the Promised Land. But we can be certain they heard about the mighty acts of God on behalf of the nation in providing food and water in the desert and protecting them from their enemies. They must have heard the tales about Yahweh punishing their parents for disobedience by not letting them live long enough to enter the land. Even if they had been young, the exploits of Joshua and the people in conquering the land consisted of miracle after miracle.

Now comes the time for Joshua to die. To the people, God says: "So I gave you a land on which you did not toil and cities you did not build; and you live in them and eat from vineyards and olive groves that you did not plant" (Josh 24:13).

If they understood that God did all those wonderful deeds, why would there be any question about whom they would serve? Why wouldn't they choose the God of miracles, the God who provided everything they needed?

Maybe it comes down to the rebellious nature inborn in all of us. Perhaps it comes down to wanting to be everything God wants us to be and still holding onto a few of the powerful pulls in our life. God says, "Let go," and we say, "Sure, except for this little thing."

When we become aware of "this little thing" that holds us back, the desire we don't want to give up, then it's time for us to pray, "Heal the parts of me that don't want to be healed." If we don't, the conflict remains. I suspect that for some of us those issues have been with us so long and have defeated us so often, we hardly recognize our struggle.

That was certainly true of me. As I walked through the months of my spiritual eclipse, I wasn't aware of being conflicted. There were things about myself I accepted as part of who I was. I hadn't liked some of those things. In the past I had prayed, and nothing happened, so I shrugged and thought, *That's who I am.* Sometimes we excuse our sinful behavior with such statements.

From my days as a pastor I vividly recall a woman named Madeline who had a terrible temper. The least little slight or a single wrong word could set her off. One day I visited her home at her request (actually she called and demanded it). She had a friend with her. Within minutes Madeline began to complain about the church. The more she grumbled, the louder and more angry her voice became as she pointed out the coldness of the congregation, the fact that she had to call me every week to get a visit, and she went down a long list of complaints. Mostly she punched me with one verbal blow after another.

I'd been through it before. Protestations only made her more adamant, so I remained silent.

"That's enough! Stop it!" her friend said. She took Madeline to task for getting angry and behaving so badly.

After a few verbal spars between them, the woman defended herself, but the friend wouldn't let her get away with it. "Rudeness has no excuse," she said.

"I have a temper. I've always had one," Madeline said, "and that's the way I am."

"It may be, but you need to get over it," her friend said.

Madeline never did. She died a year or so later—still angry and hot-tempered. Even so, her friend's advice was correct.

Just the Way I Am

When someone pushes us, we have two powerful responses. The first is, "It's something that I pray about all the time." This may likely be true, and it gets us off the hook. Who would challenge that spiritual-sounding response?

The second is closer to that's-the-way-I-am, except it's a bit more theological. "That's part of human sinfulness in me. It's something God hasn't given me victory over."

Sometimes we point to the apostle Paul's statements in Romans 7:14-15: "But I am merely human, and I have been sold as a slave to sin. In fact, I don't understand why I act the way I do. I don't do what I know is right to do. I do the things I hate" (*CEV*).

When I first studied theology, my teacher pointed out that Paul was referring to himself prior to his conversion, even though

my sincere professor could show me nothing to prove his asser-
tion. He simply couldn't believe that the great apostle could still
struggle with sin.

I didn't have any problem with those statements. Paul was a
human being; therefore, sin remained a constant reality. I like to
think that the closer he moved toward God, the more he became
aware of the unhealed places in his spiritual life. I like to think
that even Paul prayed, "Heal the parts of me that don't want to
be healed."

Perhaps I've thought a great deal about this because when
there's nothing to focus on but the absence of God's face, it's easier to look at those unhealed parts of myself. I can only say that
when it pleases God to speak to us, we need to respond and ask
for that healing. I wrote *speak,* and I mean by that when God
chooses to deal with us, nudge us, poke us or kick us.

When we enter into the divinely appointed darkness, we hear
the voice differently from other times—or at least this was my experience. It's not a thunderous cry from Mt. Sinai; it's not the still,
small voice that whispered to Elijah in the cave. It may be so subtle that we hardly know we've "heard."

For me, I have no idea when God first spoke. One day the burden was there. It felt like a slight but nagging headache that didn't
want to go away. No matter what I did, it troubled me enough for
me to remain aware of its presence. I prayed for help. But I had
prayed for help hundreds of times before over the same issue.
Nothing happened. Something inside me wouldn't allow me to
shrug and go on. I felt caught. Trapped. I had to cry out for help.
And I did, but I didn't expect deliverance.

The book of James responds to that attitude. "But when you
ask for something, you must have faith and not doubt. Anyone

who doubts is like an ocean wave tossed around in a storm. If you are that kind of person, you can't make up your mind, and you surely can't be trusted. So don't expect the Lord to give you anything at all" (Jas. 1:6-8, *CEV*).

Today's New International Version reads, "Those who doubt should not think they will receive anything from the Lord; they are double-minded and unstable in all they do" (vv. 7-8).

When we encounter the unhealed, unsanctified parts of ourselves, we need serious help. It seems to be like having someone say, "Would you like to inherit a million dollars or be fifty thousand dollars in debt?" How can we not reach for the blessings of God when they're offered to us so freely?

I don't know.

I simply know that we still hold on.

I don't understand other people and haven't been able to understand myself. We humans have the kind of nature that resists change unless God intervenes. For me the awareness of the intervention came when I heard myself say, "Heal the parts of me that don't want to be healed." I talked to God quite often that morning. I wanted to hold on to my old ways but God wanted to set me free.

"Heal the parts of me that don't want to be healed."

I don't remember how long I asked that day. I don't remember how many days I made the same request. But I know that every single day I prayed those same words.

Deliverance came. I don't know how or when. I can only tell you that one morning after I prayed those words, I realized that I didn't need to say them again. I had been healed. That desire was gone. I was free. This is another way of saying that God did for me what I couldn't do for myself. But then that's the way God's grace in Jesus Christ works anyway.

Even as I stumbled around in my darkness, I realized that God was working with me, nudging me, pushing me, making me aware of needs I hadn't taken time to observe before.

—◊—

I seemed to have no choice—
I had to focus on my unhealed parts.

20

BEYOND SURRENDER

"Just surrender everything to Jesus Christ."

I've heard those words from countless preachers. I've even said them to others on a few occasions. They're appropriate during the times we hold on and don't want to let go. What we refuse to abandon may be dreams or long-sought-after goals. The call to give them up comes when they interfere with a fully committed life of obedience.

Sometimes our desires are so strong that we can't hear God's voice telling us that those desires are leading us in the wrong direction. When we insist on what we want and then all but demand that God give us those desires, we struggle. Often that internal conflict centers on stronger pleas to "make it happen."

It often takes me awhile to accept the fact that I'm holding on and don't want to let go of a desire. The core of the struggle involves something that I've wanted a long time and consider fairly important. Those holdouts are different for each of us, and they can be anything from a work promotion to the purchase of a dream house or a romantic yearning for a particular person.

Fighting the Battle

Anyone who's been a Christian for a while has fought the battle of surrender. It finally comes down to our desires in opposition to

God's will. For each of us surrender comes about differently. For some it may happen as soon as they suspect the desire conflicts with God's will. For others the yielding takes place because they sense it's wrong, even though they don't understand the reason. The cause of giving it to the Lord isn't as important, however, as the fact that we finally say, "Yes, I give up."

Somewhere early in my Christian experience I developed a theology of surrender—and a rather naïve one at that—and yet one I've heard others speak of holding to.

Several times I wanted something badly. It's the kind of thing that implies, "If God will grant this, I can be happy." That wasn't true, because I'd always find something new to want, but such desires loomed so powerfully in my line of vision, it seemed as if my life would be miserable without them. So I held on.

I did the holding in a number of ways. Usually I prayed. If nothing happened, I'd resort to something called "praying through"—an idea and method I absorbed early in my Christian experience.

A dear, elderly Christian man named Claude Puhl was the first to talk to me about that method. He cautioned me to pray and ask God if it pleased Him for me to have it. "If you don't get no, then you pray through to yes."

Several times Claude told me, "If you want something badly enough, bombard heaven. You have to show God how serious you are. You pray when the heavens seem like brass, and you don't stop. You keep praying until the power of your petitions breaks through the barriers."

He believed that Satan or demons were out there in the atmosphere between us and heaven, acting like goalkeepers to stop our petitions from scoring a victory. I'm not making fun of Claude, and I believe there are times that is exactly the right thing to do.

In the Bible, for instance, we can look at barren Hannah, who held out for God to give her a son. Jacob wrestled all night with an angel at the Jabbok River. What about Jesus' agony when He prayed in the Garden of Gethsemane? Those are the times when we speak of heavy hearts and burdens that we can't cast off.

The difference between these examples of biblical praying, and perhaps what Claude was trying to teach me, also had to do with surrender. Just holding on wasn't the end. God blessed Hannah and Jacob. Jesus, however, prayed until He finally cried out, "Yet not my will, but Yours be done." Paul had what he called a "thorn in the flesh," which may have been a physical problem. He said he prayed three times for deliverance, but the Lord didn't deliver him.

Paul surrendered because he understood the purpose. "Therefore, in order to keep me from becoming conceited, I was given a thorn in my flesh, a messenger of Satan, to torment me" (2 Cor. 12:7).

Jesus pleaded for His heavenly Father to open a different path to follow—being a human being, He didn't want to die. In Luke 22:39-46, we read the story of His deep agony until He said, "Yet not my will, but yours be done" (v. 42).

Jesus, Paul, Jacob and Hannah had all "prayed through." They received different answers, but they exemplified the kind of petitioning Claude advocated.

"Just praying once doesn't always do it," he said. "You have to stay at it."

I listened to Claude and still remember his advice. For me the problem usually stemmed from not knowing God's will. I knew what I wanted, so that became the focus of my petitions. "Please, God, grant this to me."

Sometimes I did break through—I prayed until I felt my heavenly Father had heard me and would give me exactly what I asked for. At other times it seemed that no matter how much I prayed, nothing changed.

Then I moved on to the next step, which was surrender. I'm embarrassed to say on paper how my devious mind worked. When I surrendered, down in the deepest level of my heart lay a secret, unexpressed desire. I thought that if I gave up, eventually God would give me what I wanted. My thinking was that if I said (and meant), "All right, I can live without getting what I want," that would be the method to get what I wanted. At issue seemed to be that if I convinced the Lord and Cec that I didn't want what I asked for, and began to live without it, eventually a loving and compassionate Master would give it to me.

Perhaps it will work better if I explain it through a personal example. I'm a writer, and that's how I make my livelihood. For 15 years I made an adequate income as a ghostwriter—I actually wrote the autobiographies and other materials for people on a wide variety of topics. I liked what I was doing, but I wanted to sell some more books under my name. (The situation has now changed, but for many years professional writers didn't receive credit for the books they wrote for others. When issued, only the celebrities' names appeared on the byline.)

I didn't mind the anonymity, and for many years it was a great test for me to not be concerned over who received credit or praise for my work. Then I sensed it was time for me to move on.

I prayed for guidance. I wrote my own book proposals. Nothing happened to change things. I prayed and agonized but still no change. The worst part of the agony came about while I ventured through my dark period. My agent still sold books for me—but they were books for other people. I wanted to create *my* own books, and that desire wouldn't go away. My wife encouraged me to keep trying.

Nothing happened to change the status. I'd write my material, and no publisher bought it. But in the meantime I'd get an offer to write a book for someone else.

The agony went on and on. I'd pray and I'd plead, and I tried to pray through. Finally, weary and worn out from asking, I said, "I'm tired of this. I surrender."

I said those words as sincerely as any I've ever prayed. I felt a certain amount of peace. But for the next few days I kept thinking now that I've given it up, maybe God will give me what I want.

That didn't happen.

I'll also have to admit that the desire to write my own books kept cropping up in my heart—and maybe that should have signaled that I hadn't fully surrendered or that I had only temporarily caved in.

That back-and-forth praying went on for several weeks. Then near the end of my dark period, something happened to me.

I had awakened about 4:00 that morning and, unable to go back to sleep, I did my usual early morning ritual and went for a run. More than two years later, that morning remains vivid in my mind. Some kind of power outage had knocked out several traffic lights and all the streetlights in our area. As I ran and talked to God, I felt as if the physical surroundings fit my spiritual status rather well. Is this all I'm ever going to go through? One kind of darkness after another? Will there never be light in my soul again?

Detachment

I stopped running and sat on a curb in the dark. That's the only time I've ever done that: I just gave up. "What's the use?" I asked. I couldn't fight anymore.

As I stared at the blackness of the predawn, I thought of a song in which the lyrics talk about holding on to things like sand slipping through our fingers.

I felt exhausted. I sensed—and I'm not aware what brought this on—that this time I needed to move beyond surrender. I had to cross a frontier I had never contemplated before. I thought of a word my New Age friends like to throw around. They refer to "detaching."

Yes, I thought, that illustrates detachment—to care deeply but to hold lightly. To detach means to make my preferences known, but to leave the results in God's hands.

I realized that's what I needed to do. I didn't need to surrender—not in the way I had done it. I needed to detach; I needed to let it go in such a way that the end results made no difference to me. (Maybe that's the real meaning of surrender, but at that point, I didn't quibble over words.)

No difference? I asked. *How can it not make a difference?*

That's when I experienced detachment. Instead of a clenched fist, I held up an open, upward palm. I had detached.

In the silence of the moment—and I have no idea how long it went on—I realized that I had to drop my own desires so completely that I could rejoice if I never wrote anything again under my own name. And yet that wasn't the stopping point either.

"I'll unplug my computer and never write another word if that's what You want." It was one of those instances when I did not realize what I meant until I said the words aloud.

"Yes, yes, that's it. It doesn't mean submitting because I can't fight any longer. It doesn't mean giving in because God is too strong for me. It means leaving it, walking away, and detaching myself."

Once I realized that was the right thing for me, detaching felt simple and seemed obvious.

Quite consciously, I realized what that commitment meant. If my heavenly Father had said, "Go look for a job," I knew I would willingly do that. It no longer mattered what I did, as long as I had the assurance that I was doing what God wanted.

Detached. Cut off. Separated. Asunder. Such synonyms kept rolling through my writer's mind as I walked slowly the rest of the way home. Before I started down my driveway, I thought, *What if God does give me what I've been asking for all along?*

"It won't matter either way," I said.

My impromptu answer made me know that I had detached.

I also realized something else as I sat on my front steps and took off my running shoes. I was growing in the darkness. Things were changing for me, even though I had no awareness of a heavenly face smiling down on me.

Now what do I do? I asked. The morning had not broken through, the sun wasn't shining, and I never heard a voice say, "This is the way, walk in it."

I felt more isolated and alone than ever. "Is there never an end to this?" I cried out. "I know that I've done the right thing, but where do I go now? You know, God, this doesn't solve anything for me."

For two more days I wondered what I was supposed to do. I was almost finished with the last contracted ghostwritten book. Another three weeks and I would be out of work.

Now what?

In a strange way, I had two feelings about the situation, and they shifted frequently. At my best moments I was at peace. "This is God's business, and I'll know what to do next when the time comes." The other part of me tried to plan ahead. I thought of other kinds of work I'd get into. I didn't worry about getting a job, because I was sure I could do that. I couldn't understand what I was supposed to do.

Then I was a week away from finishing the project.

Two days away.

In the past I would have scurried into action, sought out something to write—anything—to be busy and productive. I wondered if I had anything to say to people. Had I stayed with ghostwriting rather than exposing the emptiness of my thoughts and the shallowness of my heart? After all, I had tried to sell several of my books, and each one had been turned down.

Instead of fretting, I took long walks in a neighborhood park. I'd do my running in the mornings, and in the mid-afternoon I'd shut down my computer and walk. Nothing made sense. I had detached, that much was clear, and I wasn't going to make any plans until I had a sense of direction.

I emailed three friends, wrote of my confusion and my detachment to convey where I was and asked for their prayers. *Should I give up writing?* I asked. *Did I have anything to say?* I supposed it was a self-pitying message, but I wanted to move on to the next phase of my life, whatever it was.

Only a day before I finished my last contracted project, I received an email from my good friend Linn Carlson. Linn wisely ignored all my complaints and got right to the heart of the issue: "God has you right where He wants you, in total reliance on Him. Thanks for sharing your frustrations. I want to encourage you, brother. Yes, you are a good writer! Yes, you do have something to say! God is already in the process of opening those doors for you. It will be exciting to see what He does in the coming days of your life. Hang in there, Cec! Remember, God is for you, Jesus is for you, and the Holy Spirit is for you."

I read the first sentence several times: "God has you right where He wants you, in total reliance on Him!"

That's true, I said to myself. *But it's not an answer. It doesn't show me where to go or what's going to happen. Sure it's true, but it still doesn't give me any great victory, doesn't show me—*

"Wait a minute," I said. "That's what this means, isn't it? That's where God wants me." I wish I could say I was overjoyed, but I wasn't.

The darkness of my life suddenly became even darker. *Total reliance.* Yes, that's where I was, and I didn't even know what the term meant. I didn't like the discomfort of not knowing where I was going or what was happening. But it was the right place to be.

I finished the contracted manuscript and sent it off. A few days later I had an offer to do another ghostwritten project, and I accepted it and another that followed it. *All right,* I thought, *I have detached myself; so now this is where God wants me. You speak, and I'll walk away from all this without ever looking back.*

Each day the reality that I had detached became stronger. That's what I find hard to explain. If the Holy Spirit had whispered in my ear, "This is the last thing you're ever going to write," I would have said, "Praise the Lord." *But I didn't know.*

For another six months I went from one ghostwritten project to the next. I continued to walk in the darkness and realized there was nothing I could do to get myself out of it. One morning when I was praying, I had a vision. I'm not a person who has those kinds of experiences, but I was sitting in a chair with my eyes open, and I had a visual image. I don't know if it was inside my head, but I "saw" a large, metal gate. The gates slowly swung open.

Just that and nothing else.

I knew that I had received a message from God. I sensed that the barred entrance was no longer closed—something was opening up. I had no idea what was opening, but I knew something would change.

Weeks passed and nothing happened. Yet I was at peace. Almost every day I thought of Linn's words that I was right where God wanted me—living in total reliance. I felt peace about it, and sometimes I could actually feel joyful. Whatever happened, it wasn't for me to get concerned about. I relied on divine wisdom. It didn't matter whether I wrote under my own name or ghostwrote for others. "It's all the same to me," I said. "I'm open to anything."

My agent called a few days later and said she had sold a book—and it would bear my own name. Other contracts followed; I rejoiced in every sale. I wrote *90 Minutes in Heaven* for Don Piper *with Cecil Murphey*. It was the book with Don Piper, but God had opened the gate.

At the same time, my detachment still held. I had promised God back then, and it would be harder now because I was getting more opportunities and more contracts. Even so, a part of my attention is there waiting for God to say, "Walk away."

I don't want to hear those words, because I love what I'm doing. Yet Linn was right: I'm right where God wants me. And I don't want to distort that situation.

God has me right where He wants me. As I move out of darkness,
I'm learning to live a life of reliance on God.

21

UNDERSTANDING SILENCE

The beating of the drums along with the wailing had been going on for three weeks. Every night, as soon as darkness came, we would hear the slow, pounding drums and the crying carry down the mountainside from Giribe. Shirley and I had lived in Kenya, East Africa, only a few months before we heard those terrible night sounds.

We learned that someone had died. Following their custom, after dark the Africans beat drums and wept for the passing of their lost one. For at least a week we found it difficult to sleep with the distant cacophony. But we soon became used to it. Their grieving lasted a full month.

One night I couldn't sleep. I tried every position and finally gave up. I went outside, sat on the steps and stared into the darkness. Then I realized why I couldn't sleep: It was the silence.

No noises came from Giribe. For a full month the night's silence had been stolen by the drumming. But tonight was different. I heard no animals crying out to each other in the darkness. I don't know how long I sat under a full moon and watched clouds drift across the skies. For a long time I didn't hear a sound.

As I sat there, I couldn't think of a single time in my life when I had been engulfed by total, utter silence. In a room there's always the ticking of a clock, the buzz when the refrigerator goes into a cycle, or a car driving past our house. That night, however, I strained my ears and waited. It gave me an eerie feeling, almost as if I were the only living creature on the planet. For however long I sat there, I seemed enveloped by God's presence.

Eventually I heard what sounded like the distant roar of an animal. Soon a truck passed on the road—something that rarely happened at night. Those two things had stopped the stillness, and by their interjecting noise into the world once again, they had broken the power of silence.

After I went back inside, I thought about silence. I thought more about noise, because it fills up so much of my life. I realized how uncomfortable I felt when I didn't hear something going on around me.

Years later, I encountered the silence again. This silence was worse because no response came from heaven's doors.

"Lord Jesus, it would be easier on me if I heard Your stern rebuke," I prayed many times. "If You want to rebuke me or punish me, go ahead; speak or let me know You're listening."

No answer came. I opened my Bible. Great meanings or deep insight didn't pull at me every day, but at other times I'd find verses or thoughts that would cause me to think or that would challenge me to grow. During the silent period I felt as if I might as well have been reading Sanskrit. One day I had read an entire chapter and then paused. I couldn't remember a single word. If I hadn't looked back, I wouldn't even have known where I read. I closed my Bible.

The Closed Bible

I also have to confess that for several weeks it stayed closed most of the time. Then I'd feel guilty, push myself to read a few verses or a chapter, but the lack of comprehension settled in again. Finally

I stopped reading my Bible. For another three months, other than to prepare my Sunday School lesson, I didn't open my Bible. In all the years of my being a believer, I had never done that before.

I felt enormous guilt if I didn't read; I experienced frustration when I did. It was easier not to read.

Over the next few months I mentioned my dilemma to a few friends. One woman shrugged. "I rarely read my Bible. I know I should, but I have so much going on, it's one of those things I don't do." She didn't seem concerned.

None of my friends helped, or maybe I didn't know who or how to ask. Or maybe, in the divine wisdom, no one would have been able to give me an answer. I know only that no matter where I looked, or what I did, I confronted what I call a spiritual silence.

One day I hit a particularly low spot—and I hit many such spots during the 18 months of divine stillness. I had been walking through the woods, heavy-hearted and still at the stage where I tried to figure out what I had done wrong or needed to do right to get God to speak. I remembered the warning God gave the Jews before they went into Egypt. If they disobeyed, "The skies above will be as unyielding as bronze, and the earth beneath will be as hard as iron" (Deut. 28:23, *NLT*).

When something is wrong, the obvious place to look is within. Why couldn't I hear God? What was interfering with the communication? Was God speaking, but my set wasn't picking up? Was the silence God's punishment? a sign of divine displeasure? Was this God's call to me to repent and change? Such thoughts brought further frustration because I'd been doing that for weeks. I had probed, questioned, self-examined and done every kind of introspection I knew how to do. I became aware of nothing that caused such divine stillness.

Whatever was happening wasn't because of sin or a hardened heart. God wasn't punishing me for anything. How I knew that, I can't explain, other than to say that I simply *knew*.

I didn't feel forsaken—then I could have launched into full-blown depression. That lack of reason (to me) was what made the silence so difficult and such a burden. I couldn't understand what was going on. And I told God so, even though I still had no assurance that the Lord received my messages.

The Value of Silence

At one point I finally wondered if the silence was totally God's doing, and there was nothing I could do to change the program or disrupt the silence. Years earlier I had read a novel by Chaim Potok called *The Chosen*. One of the key elements in the book revolves around a Hasidic rabbi who refused to speak to his son. The man did everything a father was expected to do except he wouldn't say one word to his boy. At the end of the book, the father breaks his silence and explains. The boy was brilliant, and the father feared that the boy would elevate himself above others and become smug and that he would never be able to understand suffering. Silence was the only weapon the father had to teach his son to have compassion for others—by remaining mute he knew he was causing pain in his son that, he believed, would one day translate into understanding and compassion.

The novel moved me deeply. I saw the value of silence. But I could hardly equate myself with the brilliant young man. The memory of that book forced me to think, and finally I asked myself, *What if God has chosen silence for a purpose? What if the portals of heaven have remained closed for my benefit?*

As I pondered the question, I couldn't find a reason that God would do such a thing. What could I learn from the silence? I couldn't grasp any therapeutic value in heavenly stillness.

I didn't give up. I thought of the mystics of old and remembered how much emphasis they put on inner calmness. So I started with them. Started is about as far as I got. After a couple hours of reading, I concluded that most of them were monks or nuns who lived the contemplative life and spent large portions of their books urging readers to renounce the world and live away from its pulls and turmoil. That wasn't the path for me.

"Lord Jesus, if I could understand what's going on," I cried out, "I could cope with this. If you'd help me figure out what's happening, I'd survive."

God didn't answer that day.

As I monitored my own prayers, I realized how much of the time I asked God to help me understand, to grasp or to know.

Silence gave me no solution. Either I had to figure out the answers on my own or—and this was much harder—give up my intense search to understand.

I opted for the latter, but it didn't solve much. Despite my intention not to ask or demand reasons, I kept doing it. I simply didn't know how to live in a world without divine messages coming at me. I had been a Christian more than half my life, and I did not know how to adapt to that new way of living. If I don't get any understanding, how do I know if I'm going in the right direction? How can I be sure I'm doing the right thing unless I know it's right?

I felt trapped again. Silence filled my ears. Nothing was going to change. I had to adjust.

"All right," I prayed, "I commit my will. I don't understand what's going on, but I'm committed." As simple as those words sound, and they probably weren't the exact words, that was one of the hardest prayers I've ever spoken. To say that it didn't matter, that I'd follow God, no matter whether I understood or was dazed with confusion, meant an intentional walking in silence.

And yet, as I thought more about it, isn't that the whole concept of relationship with God? In the Old Testament, God made covenants with individuals but mostly with the chosen nation of Israel. The covenant denoted an agreement that was a gracious undertaking entered into by God for benefit and blessings for those who receive the promises and commit themselves to the obligations this involves. This same idea appears in what we call the New Covenant. Because of Jesus' sacrifice, Christians vow to follow obediently and without reservation.

Obligations

Through the ages, whenever believers agreed to God's New Covenant, they made a commitment, and they had no idea what they were obligating themselves to.

Yes, I thought, *that's what's going on here.* When I was 22 years old, I entered into an agreement with Jesus Christ to follow, regardless of how my life went. I had no idea what such loyalty or obedience would demand. As the weaker in submission to the stronger power, I consented to the terms without reservation.

But that was before God's silence. It wasn't a great moment of insight but more like a reminder. Now I knew what I had to do. After a lengthy struggle, I finally figured out how to pray in the midst of my confusion. "God, I commit myself to you unreservedly." To pray those words wasn't difficult. The difficulty came whenever I wanted an explanation. Then I had to push away my inner demand for clarification and pray again, "God, I commit myself to you unreservedly."

After I made that commitment, I remembered having read John Flavel's *Mystery of Providence* (written in 1678). He distinguished between the secret will of God and the revealed will. He quoted Deuteronomy 29:29: "The secret things belong to the LORD our God, but the things revealed belong to us and to our children forever, that we may follow all the words of this law." Flavel believed that the first—the secret will—was God's business, and ours was to follow the revealed will unreservedly.

That sounded fine to me, yet even then I wanted to say, "But Lord, won't you at least give me a hint?"

I finally concluded that my task was to go forward, blindly if necessary. If Flavel's theory about the two kinds of divine will are correct, then it implies that it's up to God to show me my responsibility.

That was a ray of hope—slight—but it comforted me. Since I knew nothing and had nothing to guide me, I put one spiritual foot in front of the other and went on. My life was in God's hands.

The silence continued for a long time. Most of the time I could accept the divine quietness. I listened. I was committed as much as I knew how to be. As I perceived God's revealed will, I would do it.

Slowly I began to accept that silence was a gift to me from heaven. I was learning to listen more intently to the Spirit's whisper. I still hadn't understood silence—maybe I never would fully—but I was beginning to realize that silence didn't mean God's absence. The divine presence was there with me all the time. The quieter I became, the more I embraced the silence, the more of a sense of God I felt.

—⁓—

I wasn't out of the darkness yet,
but I was getting closer.

SHAPED BY SILENCE

What would it be like to live in total darkness for five months? To see no difference between night and day?

I got a hint of such a situation when I wrote Norman Vaughan's account of his 14 months as a dogsled driver in Antarctica with Admiral Richard E. Byrd, in a book called *With Byrd at the Bottom of the World: The South Pole Expedition of 1928-1930*. Vaughan fascinated me with his accounts of the never-ending days of blackness.

They landed Christmas Day 1928. He and other dogsled teams carried supplies off the ship to Little America, anxious to build living quarters and get settled. They had to get the camp ready before total darkness descended. Within four months after their arrival they knew they would live in a world of absolute darkness (except for their own electrical power). No natural light would shine during those days and nights when temperatures fell to 50 degrees below zero. They constructed a radio tower, storage spaces, as well as the living quarters with an underground tunnel to the dining room. They had all the food and supplies they needed. Besides their own electrical plant they also had radio communication with the outside world.

They had known the darkness was coming and prepared for it. Temperatures fell and the winds increased. By the first of April 1929, all natural light had vanished.

Norman spoke of what living in darkness did to some of the 43 men. One in particular became morose, depressed, began to carry a gun and threatened to kill Vaughan.

No one was immune from the effects of darkness; some held up better than others. One man kept busy making new harnesses for the sled dogs. Others read and reread every book in the communal library. The men slept long hours.

One thing all of them knew: the darkness wouldn't last, even though it felt that way at times. They waited, counted the days and dreamed of what it would be like to walk outside without fear of being lost in the blackness of the elements.

The experts had said the light would return August 20, 1929. On that day, several men climbed the electric tower. At the appointed time, their eyes scanned the horizon. Cheers went up when one man spotted the first flickers of light.

As the men watched from below, slivers of light slowly snaked across the horizon. Each day they saw a slight increase in light.

As terrible as the experience was of living in total darkness from April through August, Vaughan says they had survived the darkness. Now they celebrated and pushed aside the ordeals of the past months.

Light and Dark

Perhaps that natural attitude can help us think about light and darkness in our life. Our darkness may be a dry period, a time when we feel alone. It may be as severe as what has been called "the dark night of the soul."

Jeremiah had obviously experienced that total blackout when he wrote, "He [God] chased me into a dark place, where no light could enter. He attacked and surrounded me with hardships and trouble; he forced me to sit in the dark like someone long dead" (Lam. 3:2,5-6, CEV).

I know the feeling Jeremiah describes, even though my circumstances didn't begin to parallel his. Darkness depresses and cuts us off from the rest of life. The deeper the darkness, the greater the sense of isolation and aloneness.

Is that how Jeremiah felt? Alone? Unloved? Unwanted? He had enough discernment to grasp the reason behind the darkness. He didn't blame his failures or sinfulness. God *chased* him into darkness.

In the Old Testament period they viewed everything as coming directly from God. Perhaps such a concept can help us today if we grasp the simple truth that nothing happens to us outside of God's will. Even when we go through the deepest torments, we know God is in control.

Like Jeremiah, like Norman Vaughan, we can handle the dark nights better if we remind ourselves that they're inevitable, that they will come and that they won't last forever. We can't chart the days or know when the light will begin to shine again, but we do know it will come. Darkness follows light. But light also follows the darkness.

We may not like it, but the deeper the darkness, like those men in Antarctica, the greater we'll value the light when it returns.

That concept took me a long, long time to understand.

Waiting

The first glimpse of that truth occurred one Sunday morning in church.

"Hey, that's right!" I mumbled the words under my breath, but I wanted to shout them for everyone to hear. Pastor David Fry was in the middle of preaching his first sermon of the Christmas season, and I heard another voice speak through him—the kind that felt like a powerful index finger striking my chest.

"Waiting is the most important part of our readiness for Christmas," he said. "Our waiting is not for nothing—it is for something—a very big something. Waiting is filled with potency, because people tend to be shaped by whatever it is they wait for. Have you noticed that? When you want something badly, your whole life tends to rearrange itself around that goal. It takes all within me to resist describing to you now what being engaged is like. [He planned to marry in three months.]

"A time when your whole life rearranges itself around that goal. I am also going to resist turning to Miriam [our church pianist, who was one month from the birth of her son] and asking, 'Is it true, Miriam, that expectantly waiting will reshape your life?'

"Waiting is a significant thing, and it will affect you to your very core. A self-employed consultant, as the current project draws to a close, waits for the next contract to come. Having accepted a job in Colorado, a couple waits for their home in Atlanta to sell. The first two years of their marriage now complete, a couple waits to get pregnant. . . .

"How about you? What are you waiting for, and how is it shaping your life? Not striving for, not object-oriented, goal-reaching effort. What are you *waiting* for? How is it shaping your life?"

As Dave continued to speak, I thought of my own life over the past year. I had been seeking—at times, desperately—to see spiritual light again. In those moments I realized that my life had reshaped and reformed itself. Everything pointed toward seeing God's face shine on me once again.

Changes That Reshape

So I waited. The waiting certainly wasn't new. What had become new was that my life had reshaped itself around the fact of waiting. My lifestyle changed in several ways and for reasons I couldn't explain to myself.

On some unconscious level I was reprioritizing my life. I pushed away certain activities and embraced others. For example, I've always been a heavy reader. Since my seminary days I've read at least a book a week. Now I realized that recently I had hardly read anything outside of the Bible or Bible-related material. I'd always enjoyed and relaxed by watching TV, but one day I stared at a stack of videotapes I hadn't viewed—programs I had taped to enjoy at my convenience. Nine tapes had piled up, and for several weeks I hadn't even looked at the titles or had any desire to put them in my VCR. Yes, I was watching fewer hours of TV than ever.

Are these permanent changes? I asked myself, and I didn't know. I assumed I'd resume my reading schedule. Right then those things didn't matter. What did matter was that I allow myself to be re-formed by the Holy Spirit.

I thought back to the pastor's mention of Miriam waiting for the birth of her child. For several months, everything in her life lined up behind that single event. She learned what she couldn't do, adjusted her physical limitations, her food and exercise—all the normal happenings of pregnancy.

"People tend to be shaped by what they wait for." The more I meditated on those words, the more comforted I felt. By then I had waited for more than a year for God to speak, to guide and to show me what to do. During that seemingly endless year I hadn't focused on waiting. I simply wanted to walk in the bright light of day again and had no thoughts about my inner or outer changes.

Serious Questions

Over the next week I began to ask myself several questions. Was it possible that God was actually leading me steadily onward and

I didn't know it? Could it be that the darkness all around me was, in reality, the glorious light of divine guidance?

Perhaps those sound like rather silly questions, but the demand to understand has always ranked high in my priorities. One of my college professors used to comment on what a pragmatist I was. I had to grasp a reason for every paper I wrote in class. More than once I challenged a professor with, "What practical impact will this have on me?"

I smiled as I realized that I had, at least temporarily, pushed away the pragmatism. I hadn't seriously asked where I'd be spiritually when the Lord smiled on me again. I had become consumed with relentlessly pursuing God's hidden face. Some days I felt as if I had gotten within inches of my goal, and on other days miles separated us. The pursuit took on far more importance than eventually seeing the heavenly smile again.

What if all of these months of silence and waiting are the Holy Spirit leading me onward? I asked myself. *What if the darkness, the loneliness, the isolation, the fighting of inner demons is God's guiding hand?*

The more I meditated on Dave Fry's sermon, the more I realized how truly his message had spoken to me. God *was* shaping me through my expectations. Being open, allowing and providing for divine interventions, had already brought about changes— some of them changes I hadn't been aware of until someone pointed them out.

My thinking made me feel like the two men who met Jesus on the road to Emmaus after His resurrection. They didn't recognize the Lord, and the three of them probably spent a couple of hours together. The "stranger" talked to them about spiritual things, but they still didn't know who He was. When they stopped at an inn to eat, they urged Jesus to go in with them. Luke writes, "When he was at the table with them, he [Jesus] took bread, gave thanks, broke it and began to give it to them. Then their eyes were opened and they recognized him, and he disappeared from their sight" (Luke 24:30-31).

Only in the "vanished presence" of Jesus had they recognized how much He had taught them on that walk. All along they were being instructed, but they didn't realize what was happening.

That's the way it is! In my own life I was as blind as those two disciples. The difference, I tried to tell myself, was that Jesus hadn't come directly to me, spoken and then vanished. In fact, as far as I was concerned, He hadn't even appeared to me on the road or anywhere else.

Or maybe . . .

Jesus in the Darkness

Yes, I admitted, perhaps Jesus had come to me in the darkness, walked beside me and whispered to me, but I had been so focused on my inner turmoil that I couldn't hear. Maybe it took that Sunday morning sermon to open my understanding.

So I was back to that thought again. *What if God's Spirit has been with me all along, just as Jesus walked along the dirt road with the two disciples? What if the events in my life for the past 18 months have been divinely orchestrated to teach me a different melody to sing? To lead me down a different path? To change the shape of my life?*

I had waited. And waited. Many times I had complained about the futility of the delay. Now I asked, was it a delay?

That Sunday afternoon I went for a long walk and spent most of that time examining my life. If—and I still had to keep adding that—if God had shaped me by months of waiting, in what ways had I become different? (Still the pragmatist!) In what ways had I changed?

Yes, I admitted, I had changed—not drastically so that everyone would notice. It wasn't as if I had shaved off my curly hair and modeled the bald look.

Yes, there were little ways. Subtle. Small. The little things I became aware of in myself but others probably wouldn't notice. But they *were* changes nonetheless.

Aside from the more obvious things I've mentioned above, I also examined my list of priorities. They had changed. Shirley and I had dropped out of a number of activities (including a weekly Bible study). For more than a year I had led a group of Christian men who searched for deeper meaning, and I resigned.

Then I examined the reasons I had given. For example, I blamed the heavy traffic getting to a midweek Bible study—and it *was* dreadful. But I knew that excuse and the other excuses I gave were not the real reason: I wanted more time to myself. Even more, I *needed* more time for me. When I thought about it, I had a momentary shock. I'm the extrovert who's supposed to get charged up being with people and involving himself in activities. But now I didn't need those things as much as I needed solitude. *That* was a rather drastic change.

A Different Me

During that lengthy walk I realized that I had come to see myself differently. I didn't feel rushed or pushed to get everything done right at that moment. Confusion was still there about my life and where I was going, but that afternoon I realized that my wait had lessened my anxieties, and it had shaped me—even without my realizing it.

David Morgan came by the next morning, and I mentioned some of what I've written above. "You're different than you were a year ago," he said. "Last year at this time you were agitated, almost frantic, trying to figure things out. You were waiting, all right, but your impatience showed through. Now I sense a calmness in you."

Yes, it was an acceptance, but it was more. For me, I sensed that some of my rough edges had been smoothed. I found myself less concerned about pleasing people and more about being true to my principles.

For example, during that period of time, two different women approached me to write their autobiographies. Both of them had tremendous sales potential, but I turned them down. They weren't the kind of books I wanted to spend my time doing. Both of them were projects that involved writing about issues that I had strong personal feelings against. As a professional, I could have done them; as a disciple, I wanted more to please God than to make money with a book.

I had changed. The Spirit had reshaped part of my life.

Yes, Dave Fry had been correct: People tend to be shaped by whatever it is they wait for. That's the way our life tends to work. We wait, and we think we know what we're waiting for. Sometimes we don't know, and we get something else—something far better. Or at least different.

When I became aware of waiting to see God's face, my goal was to get through the ordeal and get back to my normal way of life. If I thought about it, I assumed that I'd be different, because every experience changes us.

This reminds me of a little sign on my bookcase, by an unknown writer, that says, "Happiness is not a station where you arrive; happiness is a manner of traveling." I thought I was seeking a destination, a place to arrive and stop. Instead, I now believe that God was teaching me a new manner of life, a way to live, a way to think, a way to communicate that was superior to what I already knew.

Peace Seeps In

After hearing Dave Fry's sermon, a sense of peace seeped into my life. For what seemed like an endless period of time, my single goal had been to have God smile on me once again, to have an awareness of a loving heavenly Father's presence. Now I recognized that in the waiting God had been quietly, secretly shaping and changing me. I was already being molded, remolded and remade by the paths through which the Spirit had led me.

Slowly the new shapes took over control of my life. And I reminded myself that they came about because of the waiting and the expectation, and most of all by the grace of God. I would be different than I had been a year earlier.

I thought of that wonderful assurance of Paul to the Ephesians, "For we are God's handiwork, created in Christ Jesus to do good works, which God prepared in advance for us to do" (2:10).

The End of Waiting

Seventeen months had lapsed since my first awareness of the darkness, and it still hadn't ended. True, in the previous month I'd seen tiny rays of light, but they flickered and were soon gone. Was I nearing the end? I sensed it would be soon.

Even though I was coming to the end of darkness, I didn't stop quoting Psalm 40:1 to myself: "I waited patiently for the LORD; he turned to me and heard my cry."

When I skimmed through my journal, the first time I referred to Psalm 40:1 was on June 5—exactly 17 months earlier. I cited that verse in my prayers every single day for the rest of the year, and every day through December, and was still doing it the following February. I don't usually quote a lot of Bible verses in my journal. Psalm 40:1 was the exception. The first phrase, "I waited patiently for the LORD," expressed my state of mind and heart more than anything else I read.

Waiting Impatiently

I had learned about the waiting that seemed to go on endlessly. In those days I lived with the first phrase and hadn't quite reached the fulfillment of the second—even though I quoted it to myself. "He turned to me and heard my cry." Conviction grew that soon I would know the Lord had turned to me.

I liked to think of the verse this way: "I waited . . . I waited . . . waited . . . I waited." If anything, the words are like a complaint—"I'm still here, God. I'm still holding on." Otherwise, wouldn't He have written something such as "I prayed, waited, and then God listened"?

Think of what it might be like for a child to be crying as the mother does another task. No matter what her focus, the cries of her child override everything else.

That concept reminds me of an incident in the Sunday School class I taught in those days. Our room was directly across the hall from the infant nursery. Occasionally we heard the muffled cry of a baby for a few seconds. One day we were in the middle of a serious theological discussion, and several babies started to cry.

Katherine Kloster, one of the new mothers, jumped up. "That's mine."

"How do you know?" I asked. "I can hear at least four of them."

"I hear *my* baby."

When she walked back into the classroom a few minutes later, Katherine smiled at me. One of the four cries had been her baby.

Mom had heard her little girl, no matter how many other voices screamed for attention.

That's my picture from this psalm. God heard the cry of a servant, no matter how many voices were out there. God didn't answer immediately—and the writer emphasizes the delay. But he also wants us to know that the waiting paid off—God did rescue him: "He lifted me out of the slimy pit . . . he set my feet on a rock" (Ps. 40:2).

Waiting and Waiting

Some psalms refer to waiting patiently, and I haven't liked reading those. I want instant response to my prayers. But, as I was learning the hard way, God was forcing me to wait . . . and wait . . . and wait for answers.

So I waited. I prayed and quoted Psalm 40:1 and waited some more. One day, however, I realized I was only mouthing the same words. They had become almost mechanical. *I'm waiting because I don't have any choice. If God left it up to me, I would have settled everything months ago.*

Perhaps more than at any other time I also realized that God had some things to do in my life, even though I didn't know what those things were. My faith said, "Complain all you want, nothing is going to happen until God's done what needs doing."

I brooded over that, even though I knew it was true. A couple of days later, I began to quote Psalm 40:1 and then added, "I wait as long as I need to for answers." I was moving on the right track, but I hadn't arrived yet.

Then, when I seemed to hit the lowest point, I called a Christian brother. "I'm going through a difficult time right now," I said. "Would you pray for me?" Quite intentionally I didn't tell him anything more. Actually I didn't know anything more to tell.

He prayed for me on the phone, then a long pause came from the other end. "You know, as I've been praying, a verse keeps coming to me." He read these words to me: "I waited patiently for the LORD." Then he said, "I feel impressed that this is a message for you."

I didn't like the answer, but I thanked him as graciously as I could and hung up. For a few minutes, I felt angry, as if God had ganged up on me. At another time I might have rejoiced to hear those words, but I didn't want more instructions about waiting. I wanted answers. I wanted intervention, help, even open rebuke, but something.

"I'll keep on praying and waiting," I promised again.

I began to feel like a character in the old *Li'l Abner* comic strip: wherever I moved, so did the rain cloud over my head. I felt as if nothing would get better or even change. Not long after my descent into darkness, Dr. Ben Campbell Johnson came to my church to present a series called "The Search for Something More." The second night, instead of preaching, Ben asked us to write questions anonymously on a card about the topic of wanting something more, and he would respond to them. My question went something like this: "I'm going through a tough time spiritually. What do I do?"

Ben read each question aloud, and when he came to mine, he read it aloud and didn't say anything while he stared at the ceiling. Then he said, "Wait." He added a few sentences to his answer, but I heard everything I needed the first time.

"Wait! Wait! Wait! What do you think I've been doing for the past year? Wait! That's all I hear from you, God. I've been patient. I've waited and—" Just then I had to smile at myself. Yes, I had waited. But I had not accepted the word "patiently"—a word I hadn't stored in my vocabulary.

Those who know me often remark that I do everything quickly. My wife says I have two speeds: very fast and complete stop. I walk fast, talk fast, think fast; and everything else gets done in double time. "Patience," I used to say, "is no virtue, so why should I ever pray for it?"

This time I heard God give me a one-word message: wait.

I waited—if I was going to follow God, I felt I had no choice. For the first time in my life I prayed for God to make me patient, to help me hold on and to believe that God would answer at the right time.

Wait Joyfully

One evening; while I was driving, I flipped across the dials to find some quiet, relaxing music. A preacher on one station arrested my attention. "So you're going through a bad time?" he asked.

"You got that right," I said aloud.

"So you're enduring, aren't you? Holding on. Trying to make it. Right?"

Yes, I thought, *you said it perfectly.*

"Well, it's not enough to endure, to muddle through, to survive the trials of life. Anybody can do that! God wants us to wait *joyfully.*"

I don't know what the man said after that.

Joyfully? How can I rejoice in the middle of this situation? That's like giving thanks to God when my stomach aches and thanking God it's not an ulcer.

I turned off the radio because I didn't want to listen to anything that preacher said. Besides, his grammar was terrible. He ended most of his statements with, "Isn't that right?" and I found his nasal tone distracting. Then I thought, *I don't like the messenger, so I reject the message. What if God wants me to hear this?*

"Rejoice?" I said aloud. "That's not the direction I feel like going."

For several minutes I drove silently, unable to escape the words that I had heard. "Is that what I need to do? Is that how I must wait—joyfully?"

It didn't make sense.

"Rejoice in the Lord always. I will say it again: Rejoice!" (Phil. 4:4). I actually heard my own voice quoting that verse.

Then another verse roared into my head: "We also glory in our sufferings, because we know that suffering produces perseverance; perseverance, character; and character, hope" (Rom. 5:3-4).

I couldn't get away from the verse. Off and on all day that verse would come to me. I didn't feel like rejoicing, certainly not glorying, so I kept pushing it from my consciousness.

That troublesome day I heard a slightly different emphasis. Paul said, "We also glory in our sufferings." Another translation says "rejoice" instead of "glory." I hurried to my Greek New Testament and, sure enough, the second translators caught Paul's meaning. Rejoice in suffering? Praise God for hard times? Does that mean that I should praise God every time something goes wrong? Rejoice when bad things happen to good people? Laugh at troubles?

Obviously not, but I did perceive something about God's way of working with me. I don't grow in simple, easy steps. If the Lord had permitted me to plot my spiritual growth, I'd have drawn a gradual ascending line that took me always upward.

The reality is that my spiritual growth looks like one of those EEG readings. My graph shows as many downs as it does ups. I also realized something—and it's slightly embarrassing to write this—but I learn some of the hardest lessons by falling on my face.

No matter how much we want to learn everything at once, the human mind doesn't work like that. Our learning curve—and its well named a curve instead of a straight line—hits plateaus, and sometimes it even goes downhill a little before it goes back up. As I've pointed out elsewhere, when things are too easy, I become complacent, and my growth stops. I need the bumps and grinds of life, even though I hate to admit it. I need them to force me to seek God's *hidden* face.

Once when my children were small, we were in Egypt on our way back from missionary service in Kenya. Our son, the youngest of the three, and then only seven years old, got momentarily separated from us on a Cairo street. People pushed past him and he didn't know what to do. From 15 feet away I could see him, but he couldn't see me. "Daddy! Daddy!" he cried out.

For the next few seconds John Mark had no thoughts about going to the pyramids at Giza or taking a ride on the Nile. His single concern was to find his daddy and be reunited.

That's how divine darkness works in my life. The Lord hides from me, and sometimes it takes awhile for me to figure out where He is. I go on momentum, on habitual action of reading and praying and attending church. Then I suddenly become aware that God isn't beside me. True, like my young son, I had wandered away; but when the shocking truth hit me, I was in a kind of spiritual panic. I felt like Mary, who asked at Jesus' empty tomb, "Where have you laid him?"

A compelling urge takes over. I must find Him. I'm on a Cairo street crying out, "Daddy! Daddy! Come to me! Help me." Of course, Daddy sees me, even when I can't see Him. Nothing is going to happen to me, but in my state of panic, I don't know that. I know only that I'm scared. I feel abandoned and needy.

Yes, I need hard times in my life.

I haven't yet reached the rejoicing-in-suffering stage. Maybe I won't ever make it, but I've progressed. At least I'm now able to say, "Thanks, God, I needed that."

I'm writing this on the other side of my experience. I'm writing at a time when God's face smiles on me and my life is going well. I'm not holding my spiritual breath and thinking, *Uh-oh, that means something will go wrong soon.* I'm enjoying this time, and I'm thankful for God's blessings.

—⁓—

Now that I'm seeing the smiling face of God again,
I know it was worth the wait.

THE LIGHT RETURNS

The end of waiting finally came—and I didn't understand at first. I awakened one morning a few minutes after 5:00, and I went out for my run. I must have hit the two-mile point before I said to myself, *Something's different. What is it?*

Then I knew. I felt wonderful. A joyfulness embraced me. My energy level peaked and I felt as if I could run 30 miles that day. I didn't increase the distance, but my pace picked up. It seemed as if my feet barely touched the ground.

"It's been so long since I've felt this way," I said to God, "upbeat feelings don't seem right."

Yes, I had finally learned to wait patiently. God had heard my cry.

Once again I quoted a verse that I had memorized and quoted to myself every day for the previous 18 months: "I waited patiently for the LORD; he turned to me and heard my cry" (Ps. 40:1). But for a year and a half I had no assurance that God had turned to me.

As I write this book, I'm long beyond that dark period. Reflecting on that time I'm so thankful that God sent that darkness into my life. However, I hope I'll never have to endure such a painful period again. And yet, if that's the only way God chooses for me to grow, I'm ready to go through another dark period.

Looking back, I realize I've learned things about myself that I didn't want to know. God has healed some of the places I didn't want healed. I've peeked at some of my shadow side and didn't like the images that filled my eyes.

And yet, I know I grew.

A Personal Postscript

I'll add this as a postscript. After I had gone through the time of the starless night and God's hidden face, my eyes did sparkle again. I found a deeper level of joy in my life. God seemed closer, more important in my life than ever before. I sensed more dependence on His grace and less of an "I can do it myself" attitude.

Only weeks after God's face began to smile on me again, I had an experience that helped me realize that not only was I on the other side of darkness, I was also different from the Cec Murphey who had been plunged into a dark hole. One Sunday morning as the others left our Sunday School class, Scott White walked over, hugged me and asked, "What's going on in your life?"

At first I wasn't sure what he meant, but he kept saying, "You're different. The classes have more depth, and you—well, you're more open to us."

He said a few more kind words, and I was so overwhelmed and unprepared, I hardly knew how to answer. Finally, in a few sentences, I explained that I had been going through a dark period, but that I had finally come into the light.

"I can see that. I think everyone in the class sees it," he said. "Your face glows."

"Really? I didn't know it showed," I said.

"Oh, it does. Your face, the way you move, the way you taught Sunday School today. Believe me, it shows."

I believed him.

—w—

I had waited a long time for the light to return.
Now I knew that it had been worth the wait.

ABOUT THE AUTHOR

Cecil (Cec) Murphey—The Man Behind the Words—has written or cowritten more than 100 books, including the *New York Times* bestseller *90 Minutes in Heaven* (with Don Piper). His books have sold millions and have brought hope and encouragement to readers around the world. Other books by Cecil Murphey include:

Christmas Miracles
When Someone You Love Has Cancer
Heaven Is Real (with Don Piper)
Everybody's Suspect in Georgia
Gifted Hands and *Think Big* (with Dr. Ben Carson)
Committed but Flawed
I Choose to Stay and *Immortality of Influence*
(with Salome Thomas-El)
Aging Is an Attitude
My Parents, My Children: Spiritual Help for Caregivers

Cecil Murphey enjoys speaking in churches and for events nationwide. For more information, or to contact him, please visit his website at **www.themanbehindthewords.com**.